A
BOLDER
PULPIT

A BOLDER PULPIT

Reclaiming the
Moral Dimension
of Preaching

DAVID P. GUSHEE
ROBERT H. LONG

Judson Press ®
Valley Forge

Bible quotations in this volume are from the HOLY BIBLE: *New International Version,* copyright © 1973, 1978, 1984. Used by permission of Zondervan Bible Publishers.

Library of Congress Cataloging-in-Publication Data
Gushee, David P., 1962–
    A bolder pulpit : reclaiming the moral dimension of preaching / David P. Gushee and Robert H. Long.
        p.   cm.
    ISBN 0-8170-1287-7 (pbk. : alk. paper)
    1. Preaching. 2. Christian ethics – Baptist authors. 3. Christian ethics – Sermons. 4. Baptists – Sermons. 5. Sermons, American.
I. Long, Robert H., 1954– .   II. Title.
BV4235.E75G87   1998
251– dc21   98–35484

*To the good people of Northbrook Church,
my fellow seekers*

— dpg

*To the wonderful congregation of
the Walnut Street Baptist Church.
Thank you for the privilege of taking my place
in the pulpit of that grand church.*

—rhl

Contents

Foreword

It seems we live in the age of ethics. People everywhere — even those who don't readily speak the language of ethics — appear to be acutely aware that contemporary life is filled with inescapable ethical dimensions. This feeling is surely not misguided. Indeed, every human being is an ethicist. Each day of our lives, we face decisions about how we should live. And we sense that rather than being devoid of significance, what we do somehow and in some way matters.

Not only do we sense that what we do matters, but we often feel as if we are being flooded with ethical questions. As a society, we feel overwhelmed by the ethical quandaries that the advent of scientific breakthroughs such as genetic engineering and the human genome project have placed upon us. As individuals, we must process an unending barrage of ethical dilemmas and choices as we are inundated with situations that cause us to scrutinize our own lives and our own selves: What should I do? How should I act? How will this decision affect who I am? Am I pleased with who am I becoming?

The tidal wave appears to have swamped our ethical shores at the very point when our society has lost its ethical moorings. The moral consensus of the past, based broadly on the Bible as it was, has been thoroughly eroded. And by and large, the church no longer exercises a pervasive influence in shaping social mores. Taken together, these developments mean that ethical questions are assaulting us at breakneck speed at a time when people no longer sense beneath their feet a solid platform on which to stand as they engage in ethical discussions and make moral decisions.

Christians are especially aware of the importance of ethical principles. We realize that to be human means to live in the presence of a God who desires that we act in a certain way. We know that our lives and actions make a difference: they count for eternity! Unfortunately, however, many Christians maintain that the ethical life is primarily a matter of "do's and don'ts" – with a special focus on the "don'ts" – and that the ethical struggle focuses on the individual Christian seeking to obey this list. This perspective gives the impression that the ethical life is a stern, austere, joyless pathway each pilgrim traverses alone en route to the glorious heavenly city.

But the kingdom ethic proclaimed by Christ does not focus on the legalistic strivings of the individual believer. Rather, the New Testament teaches that the ethical life is relational; it is life in community. Christians form a community, more specifically, a community under God. As such, we are to be a fellowship of people who have been so transformed by God's own power that our relationships show forth the divine character. At the same time, God calls us to be a community in the world, that is, to live out our community life in the midst of the world around us.

Doing so requires that we respond to life in the present and to the crucial issues of the day by drawing upon the resources of the Christian faith. Ethical living means ordering our steps in every situation of life according to the fundamental faith commitments we share as Christians. It involves putting into practice our foundational Christian commitments, living them out in the day-to-day realities of our lives. Ethical living entails being conscious of what we have come to believe about God, ourselves, and our world and then acting on the basis of these convictions. The fundamental ethical questions of "What should we be?" and "How should we live?" ought, therefore, to lead us back to the foundational question: What would it mean to live according to our Christian faith commitments in the concrete situations of life? Hence, we must ask continually, By the power of the Spirit and in accordance with the divine revelation in Jesus, how can we best live as the transformed people of God who embody the biblical disclosure of who God is, who we are, and what God's eternal purposes are? Or stated another way, in all our relationships as Christ's people, how can we embody the love that characterizes God's own life?

This understanding of Christian ethics gives new significance to the church as a moral community. It is in our life together and not in the confines of the solitary life that we come to understand and to live the ethical life. And this in turn gives new importance to the role of preaching and preachers in the community of Christ. Indeed, if we are to discover what the Spirit is saying to us as a community that gathers around Jesus Christ, we need to be instructed in the ways of God as revealed in the Bible. We need to hear repeatedly the biblical narrative and its implications for life in the present. Such biblical instruction comes through solid, forceful, expository preaching that refuses to remain merely on the cognitive level but instead issues the challenge of ethical living that is inherent in Scripture. Life-changing biblical instruction emerges as those who preach the Word also embody the biblical ethic in its many dimensions in their own lives and relationships.

By highlighting and exemplifying the significance of ethical preaching for the sake of the mission of the church, David Gushee and Robert Long have done a great service, not only to those who would be faithful preachers of the whole counsel of God but also to those whose lives can be transformed through the Spirit-empowered ministry of the Word.

STANLEY J. GRENZ
Professor of Theology and Ethics
Carey Theological College and Regent College, Vancouver, B.C.
Northern Baptist Theological Seminary, Lombard, Illinois

Preface

The primary purpose of this book is to assist ministers in the preparation of sermons related to the Christian moral life. We believe that those who preach the gospel of Jesus Christ need to think as seriously about the ethical dimension of the Christian message as they do about the gospel's theological, doctrinal, and pastoral components. Currently, however, the fields of homiletics and Christian ethics generally fail to equip ministers adequately for this component of their work. This failure is reflected in the morally truncated preaching ministry of the contemporary church and with it a variety of negative ramifications for both church and society.

Despite the increasingly voluminous body of literature on preaching, resources specifically related to the Christian moral life are scarce. Whereas the local church minister can find an abundance of homiletical materials addressing the hermeneutical, theological, doctrinal, and pastoral dimensions of preaching, the ethical dimension has been relatively neglected. A recent search of the relevant bibliography revealed only a very small collection of works that focus on the intersection of preaching and ethics. A handful of books can be found that address a single moral issue, such as the environment; a single moral theme, such as social justice; a morally significant biblical genre, such as the prophets; or particular biblical texts with moral implications, such as "the hard sayings of Jesus." There is even a work on *The Ethics of Persuasive Preaching*. But no work in Christian homiletics exists that considers in a systematic way the integration of a fully developed moral vision of Christian preaching.

Further, our sense is that most biblical commentaries consulted by preachers lack adequate discussion of the moral dimension of the texts they consider. Biblical scholars with great interest in ethical concerns, such as the wonderful and much-needed Walter Brueggemann and Elizabeth Achtemeier, are too few and far between.

As well, preaching journals tend not to build sufficient consideration of the moral dimension of preaching into their standard fare. For example, the helpful and widely respected preaching journal *Lectionary Homiletics* offers the following categories of material to assist ministers in preaching through the church year: exegesis, theological themes, pastoral implications, the lesson and the arts, sermon reviews, and preaching the lesson. No category related to ethics can be found. We undertook an informal content analysis of the last two years' worth of two of our favorite pulpit periodicals, *Preaching* and *Pulpit Digest*. While both of these magazines included articles and sermons with some moral content, only a small percentage of either articles or sermons (under 5 percent) directly tackled significant moral issues. This brief review does not mean that moral themes are always absent from these or other preaching journals, but it does signal the relative lack of attention to the moral dimension of the homiletical task. That which is not named can easily become invisible.

One would hope that the discipline of Christian ethics could be a source of help for ministers in this regard. Unfortunately, the literature of Christian ethics, though rich with moral content relevant to the church, is generally not written in a manner that is accessible to the average pulpiteer. The irony is that many ethicists desire few things more than to make an impact in the local church; many would name that as the central goal of their work. The problem is that most scholarly works in Christian ethics are written for other ethicists and assume a knowledge of the discipline that the average pulpit minister does not possess. Meanwhile, the handful of popular works in Christian ethics tend to be written for laypeople. Those few ethicists who have directed their attention in a practical manner to preachers have tended to focus on the personal moral life of the minister. While the treatment of this issue is certainly valuable – indeed, the subject will be discussed briefly in this book – that subject alone does not exhaust the morally oriented direction needed by the local church pastor.

For these and other reasons, the moral dimension of the gospel tends either to be neglected or badly mishandled from the pulpit. Many ministers simply shy away from preaching not only on particular moral issues such as racism or abortion but also on the moral dimension of Christian discipleship and Christian community, on such themes as character, virtue, moral vision, moral imagination, and moral responsibility. The outcome is a strange silence from the pulpit concerning issues of importance in the Scripture and of great concern to society as well.

When preaching related to morality does occur, it tends to have a number of deficiencies. Some of these will be outlined in the chapters that follow. We believe that the gravest deficiency, at least in contemporary American church life, is the substitution of unthoughtful and frequently uncivil politicking and posturing for actual biblical reflection on the moral life and the moral issues Christians face in society today. This occurs both in evangelical and mainline churches, on the right and on the left. It is not at all easy to distinguish political ideology with a religious veneer from authentic biblical exegesis, interpretation, and proclamation, especially in these highly politicized days. It is just about impossible without informed reflection and conscious effort. Yet few ministers appear both willing and able to engage in that effort.

Our conviction, then, is that far too few ministers adequately address the moral life in their preaching ministry, and that their failure contributes to the moral malnourishment of the contemporary church, the erosion of authentic Christian moral community, and the increasing irrelevance of the church to a contemporary culture badly in need of our intelligent engagement. Underlying this conviction is a second belief: that even in late twentieth-century, postmodern, ever-more-post-Christian America, the preaching ministry that occurs in the churches really does matter, both to the community that is the church and to the broader community we call American society. Those who believe these two things should read this book. Those who

do read it, we hope, will find here a helpful analysis of the
problem and a useful corrective.

This book is written primarily for ministers involved in the
preaching ministry of the local congregation. We have aimed
for brevity in communication and for the elimination of anything extraneous to our purpose. For this reason, we use as
few notes as possible. We intend the book to be theoretically
well grounded (in theology, ethics, Scripture, and homiletics)
but primarily practical in its orientation. In the end, we simply
want preaching ministers to have a clearer sense of the moral
dimension of their work and some tools with which to build
that moral dimension into their weekly ministry.

The book is arranged in two parts. Part 1: Method, addresses
the question of how the preaching minister can and ought
to address the moral life from the pulpit. This part begins
with an assessment and critical analysis of the current state of
preaching on morality in the contemporary North American
church (chapter 1). Chapter 2 offers a constructive proposal
concerning the moral dimension of Christian preaching. The
final chapter of this section, chapter 3, offers a model for the
development of ethically minded sermons, focusing both on
the personhood of the preacher and on the craft of morally
oriented preaching. Chapters 1 and 2 were drafted first by
David Gushee; chapter 3 was drafted by Bob Long. We worked
through each other's material, however, editing freely, and the
end result is genuinely a joint effort.

Part 2: Sermons, offers eighteen actual sermons that one or
the other of us has preached. Each sermon addresses an important moral issue or theme, such as the sanctity of life, the
environment, or ambition. Each sermon offers an example of
morally informed Christian preaching on the issue at hand;
and without being exhaustive in any way, together the sermons
touch a broad cross section of moral themes and issues.

The sermons are arranged in the sequence of their primary
biblical texts. Prior to each sermon, we include brief pre-
liminary discussion of the context in which the sermon was
preached and some of the ways in which the sermon reflects

the method outlined earlier in the book. Because each sermon included in this volume was actually preached by one or
the other of us, they were not coauthored, as were the first
three chapters, but are included as representatives of the kind
of morally focused preaching we endorse in this book. The
original preacher of each sermon is identified.

David Gushee is a professor of Christian Studies and direc-
tor of the Center for Christian Leadership at Union University
in Jackson, Tennessee, and Vice President of Evangelicals for
Social Action. His training is in the discipline of Christian
ethics. David is a graduate of the College of William and Mary,
Southern Baptist Theological Seminary, and Union Theological
Seminary (New York). During most of the time in which this
book was written, David served as interim lead pastor of an
innovative, seeker-sensitive Baptist congregation in the Jackson
area. Many of these sermons were preached in that unique
context.

Bob Long serves as pastor of the 6,000-member Walnut
Street Baptist Church in downtown Louisville, Kentucky. He
has served churches in four states over the past twenty years.
Bob received his academic training at Murray State University
and New Orleans Baptist Theological Seminary. Bob's Sunday
morning sermons – a sampling of which are included here –
are shown live on the ABC affiliate in the Louisville area and
watched by thousands of people each week.

Thus, one of us is primarily an ethicist who loves the church
and cares about preaching and the other is primarily a preacher
who loves the church and cares about ethics. Theologically,
both of us are Southern Baptists and are comfortable identify-
ing ourselves as evangelical Christians, though we would reside
in the center rather than either the right or the left of that particular slice of the theological spectrum. These denominational
and theological commitments are inevitably reflected on each
page of this volume, and surely we can speak most authori-
tatively about the contexts we know best. Yet we believe this
book will be of interest to many others who do not share these
particular commitments, and we certainly intend to address a

broad Christian audience. The responsibility of unfolding the moral dimension of the Christian gospel for the people of God rests on the shoulders of everyone who has the privilege of occupying the pulpit – Catholic, Protestant, and Orthodox, mainline and evangelical, whatever labels one might use. We hope and pray that we two Southern Baptists have offered here a book that will be of use to the whole people of God and will advance the cause of Christ both in the church and in the world.

One final note about the vexing question of language. When referring to God, we prefer to stick with biblical practice and use the male pronoun. This is certainly the standard practice in the churches we serve; it would be inauthentic to attempt to alter that language for this volume. When making reference to human beings, we use language that clearly includes both men and women. When speaking of preachers, we also use inclusive language. Finally, when employing quotations of a certain vintage, we have gritted our teeth and retained exclusive language where that exists rather than alter it in accordance with contemporary practice and our own preference.

Acknowledgments

Many people and organizations deserve thanks for their role in making this work possible. Our acknowledgments are listed separately below.

David Gushee — This book began as a summer research project that was funded by The Pew Charitable Trusts and authorized by a faculty committee at Union University. I am grateful to both Pew and to this committee for their confidence and support.

I offer my thanks to the library staff of Union University, who worked long and hard to gather the many materials used in this research that were not available on site. David Sutherland and Sheri Lovett, Union student assistants, provided invaluable help. My gratitude goes out to both of them. I am grateful to Mike Duduit, editor of *Preaching*, for his insights and bibliographical leads, as well as for giving me access to his archives.

I thank my precious wife, Jeanie, who has listened supportively to nearly every one of my sermons, some of them more than once!

Bob Long — I thank Judy, my wife, for her unfailing love and friendship, without which nothing I could ever say about the preaching event would matter.

I thank my daughters, Valarie, Veronica, and Victoria, for their love and devotion. They make Dad feel very special because they believe in me.

And I thank my friend and coauthor, David Gushee, for his encouragement and the flint of his intellect, which sharpens the flint of my own thinking.

Both of us are grateful to our families for their willingness to share us with this project.

Finally, we both want to express our deep gratitude to the congregations with whom we serve: Northbrook Church (David) and Walnut Street Baptist Church (Bob). Thanks for listening to our sermons even when they are not profound or artful. Your weekly hunger for the truth of the gospel is our continuing inspiration.

Part 1

METHOD

CHAPTER ONE

A Strangely Distorted Voice

The Moral Vacuum in Contemporary Christian Preaching

Time for confession: we have been silent. The pulpit has been tame and the pew timid. We Christians have been speechless....Fact is, nowadays, the church is running flat-out scared, trying to hold onto public approval in a crumbling age....Look, is there anything worse than the strange strangulated sense of "I should have spoken"? To live on, knowing that we missed the moment when we should have spoken. So, can we confess? We have been silent, a "silent majority" church. We should have spoken.
— DAVID BUTTRICK, 1987[1]

We write this book because we believe that David Buttrick is right. The pew is timid, the pulpit tame, the church largely speechless when it comes to addressing the moral dimension of Christian proclamation. This speechlessness creates a gap in Christian proclamation, a vacuum that needs badly to be filled. It needs to be filled because the biblical witness demands it, the church's fidelity requires it, and the world's need cries out for it. We write in an attempt to show how this vacuum might be filled.

The Moral Dimension of the Gospel Message

We need to be clear from the outset exactly what we mean when we speak of the moral dimension of Christian preaching.

Here we will outline our meaning and its underlying assumptions and convictions in a few broad brush strokes, saving further consideration for the next chapter.

The gospel of Jesus Christ addresses human beings at every level of their existence. Christ is the Savior of the *world* (John 3:16). Through the Holy Spirit, every aspect of the human person is to be transformed (Romans 12:1–2). Spiritual, moral, intellectual, psychological, and emotional dimensions of human personhood are all at stake in the gospel message. Likewise, the gospel – rightly understood – addresses human communities and human societies with its word of redemption. Thus, it is fair to assert that proclaimers of the gospel should regularly address all dimensions of human personhood and human community that the gospel itself addresses. To fail to do so is to proclaim an incomplete gospel, leading ultimately to infidelity to the preacher's mandate.

In the preface we employed a variety of terms to describe that aspect of the gospel, and thus of preaching, that we want to consider in this book: "the Christian moral life," "Christian morality," the "moral dimension of Christian existence/ discipleship," and so forth. By all of these terms we mean the following: *the Spirit-empowered effort on the part of the disciples of Jesus Christ to discern and to practice a way of life that conforms to the will of God and advances the kingdom of God.* This is a formal way of articulating the moral dimension of Christian existence. This dimension of life has to do with who we as Christians fundamentally are (moral character), what kinds of decisions we make, and how we go about making them (moral decision making), what kinds of goals we embrace (moral intentions), how we see the world and its possibilities (moral vision/ imagination), how we conduct ourselves (moral practices), and more – nearly every aspect of living is in some way related. These various dimensions of Christian character and conduct are demonstrated and worked out in various arenas of life: in individual life; in families; within the community of faith; and in Christian engagement with the world of culture, politics, and society. This, essentially, is what we mean by the moral dimension of Christian existence. And it is this dimension of life that we think preachers need to do a better job of addressing.

Notice what we do not mean by this term. We do not restrict Christian morality to moral decision making concerning "quandaries" (agonizing choices) that people face, even though we do face such choices at times. We do not restrict it to controversial contemporary moral issues such as abortion, race, and homosexuality, though addressing such issues is indeed a part of the overall task. We do not restrict this moral aspect of existence to knotty issues of professional ethics in law, business, medicine, and so on, though certainly the lawyers, businesspeople, and medical professionals in our congregations would rejoice if we could offer them some help. Likewise, we do not restrict our scope to individual morality nor solely to the realm of inner attitudes and motives. All of these are common misunderstandings of the meaning of Christian morality – that is, they are misunderstandings if they are understood to exhaust the content of the Christian moral life. Instead, Christian morality involves both character and tough choices, both "hot potato" issues and quiet and perennial concerns, both professional conundrums and congregational moral well-being, both individual, inner struggles and corporate, social evils.

We believe that every book of the Bible and just about every biblical passage (even most of the genealogies!) has a moral dimension. Likewise, it seems obvious that the daily life of the people in our pews cannot fail to have a moral dimension, for that is the reality of human life. Every day, both individually and corporately, character is formed and tested, quandaries arise, social issues impinge, moral decisions must be made. Some days the moral dimension of life is obvious and pressing; other days it flows quietly beneath the surface. Yet the classic biblical question – "How shall we then live?" – is and ought always to be in the consciousness of our churches and the people who constitute them. For the preacher, whose task is to move between the biblical text and the contemporary world, both Scripture and daily life demand that we attend to this question in our weekly preaching ministry.

The challenge facing every preacher, then, is to find a way to integrate this moral dimension both of life and of the gospel into the weekly preaching ministry. This is not an easy task, as many can attest. Other aspects of personhood, Christian community, and the gospel message need to be addressed. We need to attend to evangelism, to doctrine, to pastoral needs, to the rhythms of the church year, to liturgy, and to worship – not that any of these are bereft of their own moral dimensions or should be set in opposition to the moral. Some Scriptures lend themselves to moral reflection better than others. We have a variety of goals in mind, depending on our congregation's needs. We face many other obstacles. But the conviction of this book is that "moral dimension preaching," while not the whole of the homiletical task, is also not a dispensable component of it. It is also our belief that this slice of the homiletical pie, so to speak, has been undercooked (now that's a tasty image!), primarily through sheer neglect and sometimes through the articulation of a politicized and thus distorted moral vision.

Excursus: Documenting the Problem

We need to say a word about documentation before proceeding. We are arguing in this book that a problem afflicts the North American pulpit and it must be addressed. The question is how we know that such a problem exists.

Our initial basis for making this claim is, frankly, anecdotal. Both of us listen to a lot of sermons – some of them our own. Together, we have listened to sermons for eight decades or so. We agree without hesitation, on the basis of this experience, that a moral vacuum exists in the preaching of the church.

We have also tried this thesis out on friends, colleagues, publishers, and others. The initial writing of this project, as noted in the acknowledgments, was approved and funded by The Pew Charitable Trusts through a diverse faculty research grant committee representing a range of universities, disciplines, and confessional traditions. That committee, on the basis of a much broader range of church experiences than the two of us represent, also agreed with the thesis that animates this project.

We have delved rather deeply into preaching literature: sermon collections, homiletics texts, preaching magazines, and so on. In that exploration we have found the following broad patterns that support our thesis:

1. Homiletics textbooks do not usually devote specific attention to the moral dimension of preaching.

2. Sermon collections infrequently contain morally focused sermons.

3. Preaching magazines and other guides for preachers do not regularly build the "moral slice" of the homiletical task into their basic fare.

Further, the one recent study we have seen that attempts to review empirical studies of preaching has found that only 5 percent of sermons deal in thorough ways with social issues.[2] We recognize that even this evidence is not conclusive. No one can fully document the content of the preaching that occurs in the thousands of churches open each Sunday across North America. The preaching literature we have reviewed represents the work of a very small slice of the most influential preachers and homileticians; and even there, as we have said, the ethical dimension is relatively weak. We firmly believe that it is only weaker at the grassroots level, albeit, with significant denominational and congregational variations and some notable exceptions – for example, in the black church tradition, in which the moral dimension of preaching tends to be much better developed.[3] Thus, we believe the evidence for our thesis is adequate enough for us to proceed. Even if we are misreading the situation to some extent, no one could argue that our nation's preachers would not benefit from enhanced attention to the moral dimension of the gospel and from the kind of help in doing so that this book aims to provide.

The Problem with Preaching

Silence

The primary problem with contemporary preaching is its silence in regard to the moral dimension of the Christian gospel. We believe it is the single most neglected dimension of the Christian message as proclaimed from our nation's pulpits.

We are not saying that the moral dimension is completely absent. The preaching literature reveals some attention to moral character, the way of life of the community of faith, and less frequent forays into contemporary moral issues. Likewise, some preachers and homileticians have much greater sensitivity to such issues than others do. But on the whole, the contrast between the moral witness of the Scriptures and the moral proclamation from the pulpit is striking. It is a deafening and profoundly troubling silence.

This silence takes various forms and manifests itself in various ways. Most broadly there is an absence of *moral vision* in today's preaching. It appears that all too few of those who occupy our pulpits do so with any conscious hope of, or plan for, communicating a moral vision grounded in the Scriptures and applicable to contemporary life. Preachers usually have an evangelistic vision, and/or a pastoral vision, and/or a doctrinal vision, perhaps even an aesthetic vision. But few seem to have a well-developed moral vision. This is the one aspect of the gospel message to which few pulpiteers or homileticians pay much sustained attention.

Second, there is the noticeable development of a canon within the canon that systematically excludes some of the most morally significant material in Scripture. Ministers working in nonlectionary traditions are especially susceptible to the proclamation of a truncated canon due to their freedom to choose their own texts week by week. In these traditions we observe that the most frequently omitted blocks of Scripture are the Prophets and the moral teachings both of Jesus and the writers of the Epistles. Speaking of the significance of the Prophets in preaching, Frederick Buechner says:

> Nobody before or since has ever used words to express more powerfully than they our injustice and unrighteousness, our hardness of heart, our pride, our complacency, our hypocrisy, our idolatry.... These particular truths that the prophets speak were crucial for their own times and are crucial also for ours, and any preacher who does not speak them in his own right, naming names including his own name... runs the risk of being irrelevant, sentimental, a bag of wind.[4]

The exclusion of the Prophets and other morally focused biblical materials leaves a shredded Scripture and an incomplete proclamation of the gospel. It is not coincidental that the preaching literature emerging out of the morally stronger preaching of the black church constantly emphasizes the centrality of the Prophets and the preaching of Jesus. Indeed, some of that literature essentially identifies the role of the preacher with the role of the biblical prophet.[5] While this identification may be questioned, its intent is welcome, especially in light of an overall pulpit landscape in which prophetic and other morally demanding texts are largely ignored.

Third, one notes a deafening silence when it comes to the moral implications and dimensions of many biblical texts that are addressed. Thus, for example, while the book of Genesis is frequently preached, rarely are the moral dimensions of the primeval history systematically explored. Yet Genesis 1–11 is full of rich material concerning God's moral ordering of creation and of human life in such areas as marriage, male/female relations, sexuality, creation, work, and stewardship, as well as important reflections on the human moral situation after sin enters the picture.[6] The same thing happens in interpretation of the teachings of Jesus when they are spiritualized in the service of a particularly otherworldly rendering of the gospel. Thus, Jesus' moral teachings do not apply now, or in public life, or apply only to inner attitudes. Here we witness silence on the one hand and a perilous distortion on the other.

Fourth, there is a remarkable silence from many pulpits concerning the moral issues of our time. It is no less than amazing how detached the contemporary pulpit frequently is from the most pressing moral issues of our day. This particular kind of silence appears to have been what prompted David Buttrick's comments quoted in our opening paragraph. Given the timing of those comments, one thinks of the heightened fear of nuclear war that was so prevalent around the world in the mid-1980s. We lived – and, in fact, still live – in the valley of the shadow of thermonuclear death. Yet how many preachers addressed (or address) that issue? Earlier, in the 1960s, Martin Luther King spoke eloquently to the issue of silence in his devastating critique of the silent, gleaming white churches in the South that stood on the sidelines, at best, during the fight for black freedom and equality. One of the greatest struggles for justice in this nation's history occurred right under the noses of the white church, which at best responded with ignorant noninvolvement. King said:

> I have traveled the length and breadth of Alabama, Mississippi, and all the other southern states.... I have looked at her beautiful churches with their lofty spires pointing heavenward. I have beheld the impressive outlay of her massive religious education buildings. Over and over again I have found myself asking: "What kind of people worship there?... Where were their voices of support when tired, bruised, and weary negro men and women decided to rise from the dark dungeons of complacency to the bright halls of creative protest?"[7]

Today many are noticing the threat of environmental disaster. While opinions differ concerning the exact seriousness of this threat or the imminence of disaster, no thinking person can deny that a significant problem exists, a problem that casts a shadow over the entire human future. Yet all too few ministers or homileticians have addressed this issue.[8] A host of other neglected moral issues of our day could be named. The Swiss theologian Karl Barth reportedly liked to say that Christians need the Bible in one hand and the newspaper in the other. When those who exposit the Bible give no evidence of awareness of what is in the newspaper, and of the relevance of the Bible to what is in the newspaper, the church becomes morally malnourished and increasingly irrelevant, even to its own members.

The black Baptist preacher J. Alfred Smith has spoken bitingly of the problems we are discussing. "Preaching on social issues is taboo among many popular preachers. They recoil from addressing social issues with the skill of persons fleeing from dangerous serpents.... They [talk] incessantly in 'perpetual Sunday twaddle' in a multitude of words which have little of the bite of reality about them because they correspond to nothing in the real world."[9] Smith offers an insightful list of the types of "bland preaching" that reinforce "status quo conformity": peace of mind; the prosperity gospel; self-esteem; Jesus as the supplier of every need without explaining how Jesus supplies human needs; cheap grace; a legalistic gospel of duty; dogma unrelated to life; proof-texting; personal piety alone; Old Testament preaching focusing on prophecy, typology, and dispensationalism; and New Testament preaching covering a limited number of themes and texts. Borrowing a thought from Alvin C. Porteous, Smith rightly calls such preaching "pious profanity" – "in that it takes the Lord's name in vain."[10]

Politicization

The second problem with contemporary preaching is politicization. To their credit, some preachers – including many of our most prominent pulpiteers, whose faces one regularly sees on television – have moved out of the silence of which Smith spoke into rapt attention to the moral issues of our day. They are speaking of Christian moral responsibility in a world such as ours. This change would seem to constitute progress. Unfortunately, a significant number of these preachers give every indication of approaching the moral dimension of the faith through the lens of political ideology rather than the Scriptures. This occurs both in liberal and conservative churches, both on the left and on the right. Though the right-leaning preachers currently have a bigger platform, from personal experience we can attest that the phenomenon does occur on the left and is no prettier there. The move from silence to speech frequently has been unaccompanied by genuinely biblical reflection on the issues at hand. The result is disastrous, both for the church and for the society the preacher is seeking to change.

One mark of politicized preaching is biblical eisegesis rather than exegesis. The preacher ascends the pulpit with a prefabricated political agenda or a particular stance on an issue to promote. He (or, rarely, she) finds a text from the Bible. Then the text is read to say what the preacher's political agenda needs it to say, or read and then dropped from the scene as the shouting begins. Sometimes this process appears to be quite conscious; more frequently it is quite unconscious, simply reflecting the pervasive impact of the political ideology brought into the interpretive process. For it is indeed extremely difficult to disentangle the strands of our most deeply held convictions and to discern which reflect culture and self-interest and which are authentically scriptural.

Another sign of politicized preaching is the drift into partisanship and incivility. The pulpit loses its freedom as it merges ever more closely with the agenda of one or another political party. It becomes the platform for attacks, sometimes quite vicious, on particular individuals representing different political perspectives. Sometimes partisan political figures are invited to use the pulpit directly for this purpose. The sense that it is important to guard the boundaries that exist between preaching and politics, between the church and the political process, is lost. Thus, the pulpit loses its independence and integrity, and a distorted message is proclaimed.

A version of this concern is articulated in an interesting way in the important book by Bryan Chapell, *Christ-Centered Preaching: Recovering the Expository Sermon.* Chapell, who serves in an evangelical context, refers with unease to the prevalence of moral exhortation, cultural critique, and societal reform messages in contemporary evangelical preaching. His fear is that while "challeng[ing] the evils of the day" is a legitimate task of the preacher, it is all too easy for the centrality of Christ's redeeming work to be lost in the midst of this effort. What results when this occurs is a "well-intended but ill-conceived legalism that characterizes too much evangelical preaching." He urges preachers to replace "futile harangues" with "Christ-centered preaching."[11] His comments are well placed. The problem is of sufficient seriousness that one is tempted to agree with J. Alfred Smith when he writes, "Perhaps these [bland preachers] are better than those angry fire and brimstone preachers who are against the world and whose sermons on social issues are characterized by 'negative bashing.'"[12]

So this is the challenge that faces those who serve the American church at the close of this century: to acknowledge the strangely distorted moral voice of the American pulpit — mainly silent, sometimes politicized — and to rediscover a healthy preaching ministry in its moral dimension.

A Diagnosis of the Problem

In this section we suggest several reasons why contemporary preaching falls so short in its treatment of the moral dimension of the gospel. We do not here offer a program for addressing all of these particular concerns; in a sense, they speak for themselves. Our own alternative approach will be outlined in the next two chapters.

Plumbing the Moral Dimension: A Difficult Challenge

The first reason for this problem with preaching is simply this: It presents a difficult technical challenge.

Consider for a moment the matter of preaching on moral issues. This is not the whole of the moral task in preaching, but it is an important part of it. Abortion, euthanasia, sexuality, marriage and divorce, the environment, war, religious liberty, patriotism, race, genetic engineering, poverty, child abuse – this is but a fragmentary list of some of the many moral issues that could and should be addressed from the pulpit. The first difficulty is the sheer number of such issues. As Jesse McNeil put it nearly forty years ago: "Multitudinous and omnipresent are the moral decisions modern man must make in the grey areas of contemporary life."[13] Many seminarians and preachers have commented to us on the overwhelming nature of the task once one begins to consider seriously the moral dimension of the gospel and the moral issues we face today. Where does one begin to dive into such a massive set of problems and issues?

Related to this problem is a second one, the matter of complexity. Every one of these issues is complex. Each is complex not only in terms of the theological and biblical issues that it raises, but especially with regard to the relevant technical information. The literature on any one of these issues, such as euthanasia, is vast. Gaining mastery over that literature and a sense of sure-handedness with the medical and scientific data involved is a significant challenge, to say the least. Similarly, as Kelly Miller Smith notes with regard to the issue of racism, sometimes ignorance related to the life conditions and life experiences of other groups lies behind the pulpit's silence.[14] Many local church ministers come to believe that they do not have either the time or the background to overcome this ignorance, and they do not want to wade foolishly into waters that may drown them. Thus, many steer clear of such issues altogether.

Finally, moral issue preaching, in particular, presents technical preaching challenges, in part due to the very complexity just discussed. It is difficult to distill the key biblical insights and factual information on these issues down into a single twenty to twenty-five-minute thematic sermon. Likewise, many of these issues are hard to treat in detail if one is committed to some models of expository preaching in which only issues arising directly out of particular biblical texts can be addressed. Indeed, rigid commitment to such an approach makes it basically impossible to address the newest moral issues, such as genetic engineering or cloning, which were inconceivable at the time of the writing of the Bible. These are real and not illusory challenges to the preacher, yet they can be overcome. We will address issues of sermon preparation and form further in chapter 3.

Existence of a Training Vacuum

Most ministers receive instruction in preaching at a theological seminary. Some get their training at a Bible college. A significant minority, especially in rural areas, never receive any formal theological or ministerial training at all. These quite likely model their own approach to preaching after other ministers they deem to be skilled practitioners of the craft.

Our concern here is with the formal training in preaching that is offered to budding preachers, especially in theological seminaries. It is our observation that in such settings Christian preaching is most frequently understood as one of the practical arts of ministry, like presiding at a Communion service, performing a wedding, or organizing a Sunday school class. In other words, it is separated in the curriculum from instruction in the classical "body of divinity" – Bible, theology, church history, ethics – that is offered elsewhere in the seminary. It is viewed as a practical skill, as a technique into which future preachers need to be initiated. There is strong emphasis on sermon building, methods of preparation, the use of illustrations, various structures for sermons, voice modulation, and so on. For this reason, seminaries frequently employ local or retired pastors to offer instruction in these classes.

The technical dimension of preaching is indeed of critical importance. Effective communication skills and strategies are indispensable if the gospel message is actually to be heard. However, it is a grave error to emphasize technique at the expense of content.[15] Far too often have we heard technically sound sermons that were utterly devoid of any substantive theological or moral content. The preacher is first a theologian, and in our view, an ethicist. A rich and deep theological/moral understanding of Scripture and of the gospel must exist if Christian preaching is to be, in fact, Christian. Preaching is not solely or even primarily a technique. One is reminded of theologian Karl Rahner's comment about religious studies academicians, which applies equally well here: "They keep on refining their methods and constantly sharpening their knives but no longer have anything to carve."[16]

The same problem exists in certain other "practical" or "technical" ministry areas, demonstrating the breadth of the concern we are articulating. Thus, departments or schools train ministers of youth or education who sometimes know how to organize a weekend retreat or a discipleship program but have no content to offer when actually leading such programs. They may be masters of group dynamics or organizational flow charts but not of the gospel's meaning. We strongly side with those who argue that seminary education must primarily focus on thoughtful reflection on the body of divinity. Ideally, instruction in practical skills related to communicating and transmitting this body of divinity would be integrated into the entirety of the curriculum. In any case, we think one source of the weakness of preaching in the area of ethics has to do with inadequate training at the seminary level: in theological education broadly, in ethical instruction particularly, and in the integration of theology and ethics into the preaching ministry. The result of this problem is ignorance or distortion of the moral dimension of the gospel.

Job Insecurity, Careerism, and Fear

Another key reason for this moral vacuum may hit a bit closer to home: fear. Ministers who dig too deeply and preach too clearly on the moral dimension of the gospel may find themselves at risk of losing their jobs or of paying some lesser but still very real kind of career price for their integrity.

The potential cost of courageous proclamation of the divine Word is apparent as early as the Old Testament prophets. One need only remember the kind of perils that men like Elijah and Jeremiah faced as they fulfilled their prophetic callings, or consider that the gospel cost the lives of nearly all of the church's earliest leaders, or recall the horrendous persecution of Christians and their leaders that continues today in many parts of the world. No one wants to experience such things.

Likewise, we live in a time of profound ministerial job insecurity. This is particularly the case in certain denominations, such as our own Southern Baptist Convention, in which preachers serve at the pleasure of their congregations alone and are thus always "only a business meeting away" from dismissal. Columnist Terry Mattingly recently wrote that every month in the United States 1,300 pastors are forced to resign or are "terminated," that nearly 30 percent of ministers have been fired once, and that in ten years 40 percent of ministers will be in another line of work.[17] An astonishing recent headline in the Baptist press declared: "SBC churches fire one pastor every six hours."[18] These days the ministry is a pretty dangerous way to make a living and especially to support a family. All of us have our own horror stories in this regard. Addressing sensitive moral issues in a rapidly changing culture, even sometimes challenging the congregation to bring their behavior into line with biblical standards, is a sure way to heighten the risk of conflict, rejection, or dismissal. As Helmut Thielicke wrote concerning American ministers some thirty years ago: "The temptation to be opportunistic, to compromise, and to cover up is always near."[19]

A seminary professor once told one of us the story of a Southern Baptist minister whose courage cost him his job and very nearly cost him more than that. He had attended the 1954 Southern Baptist Convention meeting in which the assembled "messengers" approved a resolution supportive of the Supreme Court's recent *Brown v. Board of Education* decision ordering the integration of the public schools. He returned to his congregation, flush with pride that the denomination had taken this progressive step, and told them of his positive appraisal. Immediately the chairman of the deacons stood up and called for the congregation to go directly into a business session. They did so and on the spot dismissed the pastor for his sin of supporting school desegregation. Moreover, he was instructed to remove his family and their possessions from the parsonage during the course of that very Sunday afternoon "if he knew what was good for him." They drove out of town as quickly as possible, stopping only at his mother's house a couple of hours away; she promptly informed him of her outrage at his stance and kicked him out of her house as well. Eighteen hours later, in shock and unemployed, he and his family arrived at the home of his former seminary professor in search of refuge.

This nauseating tale reminds us that faithful gospel preaching may cost the preacher quite a bit. But this does not relieve the preacher of his or her obligations, for the call to ministry is a call to risky service in the way of the cross. Risk is part of the meaning of our ordination vows. Certainly we need to be "wise as serpents" in choosing how and when to speak a courageous word from the pulpit and be careful not to browbeat our congregation or to address issues without adequate sensitivity or preparation. But we need to recover the courage of our vocation, rejecting the temptation of careerism or the overweening power of raw fear, both of which distort our approach to the Christian gospel. On the one hand, as David Buttrick put it, "We have been silent" long enough, causing us to blatantly ignore our moral obligations in the pulpit, overlooking both obvious moral wrong and basic biblical teaching. On the other hand, to win political and congregational support, we have sometimes offered moral preaching but have "played to the crowd" rather than faithfully adhering to the Word. Let us give the great Swiss theologian Karl Barth the final word on this subject:

> Woe to the minister who does not see that the Word has a real significance for the men of today. But that man is even more to blame who recognizes what the Bible has to say to modern man, but is afraid of causing scandal and thereby betrays his calling. The Word confronts modern man, to disturb and attack him in order to lead him into the peace of God. This Word

must never be distorted or obstructed by laziness or disobedience. The preacher, therefore, must have the courage to preach
as he ought, courage that does not flinch from a direct attack
and is unmoved by the consequences which may result from his
obedience.[20]

Moral Tone Deafness

It may simply be that the moral vacuum of the contemporary
pulpit reflects the moral "tone deafness" of large segments of
the church itself at this time in history. Many Christians and
congregations simply have a "tin ear" when hearing the moral
dimension of the gospel message.

There are many reasons for this inability to hear or to hear
rightly. Especially in the white evangelical circles with which
we are most familiar, a morally truncated rendering of the
gospel message is widely, though not usually intentionally, embraced. The Bible is understood to be the story of personal
salvation and admission to heaven through the atoning sacrifice of Jesus Christ. Human response essentially begins and
ends with assent to belief in Jesus. The church's mission consists solely in telling others this story in order that they might
be saved and gain eternal life. Thus, the preaching in such
churches almost exclusively consists of repeatedly retelling the
story of Christ's sacrificial death in order to "win souls." While
this depiction may seem like a caricature to some readers, in
our experience it is a quite fair summation of the life and
work of many churches.[21] And it is rooted, as Arthur Van Seters
has noted, in a broader Christian privatism that represents a
capitulation to those modern intellectual trends that pushed religion into the private sphere some three centuries ago. "With
the emergence of the industrial world, mechanistic compart-
mentalization separated interconnected parts of society and set
religion in a corner."[22] This kind of religion would deal only
with the private, inner, and affective dimensions of life.

Such an understanding of the gospel cannot help but create and then reinforce, generation by generation, a morally
unreflective Christian ethos. Congregations of the saved grow
accustomed to hearing the basic salvation message again and

again. Ministers grow accustomed to preaching such messages. Biblical texts replete with moral implications are instead mined for their (narrowly understood) evangelistic possibilities alone. Other texts with obvious moral impact are simply ignored. Such patterns of interpretation become deeply ingrained. Thus, the story of the rich young ruler (Matthew 19:16–29 and parallels) is preached as having nothing to do with money, wealth, or greed but is solely about one's rejection of the offer of salvation. Hence, the fundamentally moral message of the Old Testament prophets is silently clipped from the canon. After a while, the average minister simply does not think about the broader rendering of the meaning of the gospel, and, if he or she does, is frequently met with bewilderment – "it's time to get back to preaching the gospel, pastor!"

Of course, it is impossible for a congregation not to have some kind of moral ethos, for functional standards of character and conduct are part and parcel of any human community. As many have observed, nature abhors a vacuum. We observe that the most common pattern in evangelical churches, for better or for worse, is for the moral climate to consist of a hodgepodge of inherited and rarely discussed personal moral norms combined with broad local, regional, or national cultural values. Thus, to take our own Southern Baptist context as an example, historically there has existed an informal but very real Baptist Christendom mentality, in which moral norms focus on abstinence-based personal moral standards: Baptists abstain from such things as alcohol, drugs, dancing, cursing, nonmarital sex, and so on. This has then been combined with a deeply enculturated, uncritical "God and country" conservatism that functions (very poorly) as a social ethic. Christian moral concern in this context consists of a quest for personal abstemiousness and freedom from the vices just listed. No social concern is to be found, no social change agenda, no critical mindedness – on the whole, a very limited moral vision. Much about it is commendable, but it is not a full-orbed biblical morality. This cramped moral ethos can and often does exist without any preaching at all to reinforce it or any fresh thinking to either challenge or confirm it. It is simply "in the air." Perhaps our readers from other traditions can substitute their own examples. The result is a moral tone deafness that exists because the moral dimension of the gospel message is not explored from the pulpit or anywhere else.

Cultural Polarization

In the past two decades or so, as we noted above, the problem of silence related to the moral dimension of the gospel has been augmented in some sectors of the church by a new problem: the preaching of a politicized gospel suitable for use in culture wars.

In one sense, the source of this problem is the same as that discussed in the last section. Nature abhors a vacuum, and thus some kind of moral ethos will exist in a church. If that moral ethos is not consciously developed by the preaching and teaching minister, it will be supplied from somewhere else. The most likely candidate for supplier is the broader culture.

Therefore, it was probably inevitable that the cultural polarization of American society since the 1960s and 1970s, which is perhaps the most significant cultural development in this nation in the latter third of the twentieth century, would find its way into the pulpit. In the absence of a coherent and authentic moral vision of the gospel message, a moral vision was supplied by the cultural warriors of both the left and the right. On both sides, much of this preaching was reactive, a hurling of volleys across the barricades at the other side, sometimes in a manner indistinguishable from playground name calling. In no sense is this culture wars-type preaching anything like authentic gospel proclamation. Pity is due the congregations on either side that have had to suffer through it.

Conclusion: The Priority of Grace

As we conclude this chapter, we want to be clear about something we are not saying. Our concern for the moral dimension of Christian preaching does not imply a belief in its primacy over what James and John Carroll rightly call "the scandal of grace."[23] While we do not agree with Karl Barth that "the only reason for preaching is to show God's work of justification,"[24] we do believe that this is the *primary* reason for preaching. Frederick Buechner draws a distinction between the "particular truths" we must preach, on the one hand, and the "gospel truth," on the other.[25] The latter is the "too good not to be true" news of God's grace in Jesus Christ. Dietrich Bonhoeffer attempted to make this same distinction through use of the terms *penultimate* to refer to ethics and *ultimate* to label God's justifying grace in Jesus Christ: "Justification by grace and faith alone remains in every respect the final word.... It is for the sake of the ultimate that we...speak of the penultimate."[26] Christian living is to be a response of the highest moral seriousness to a God who has taken the initiative of grace toward us. But that divine initiative comes first.

Thus, our argument in this book is about the penultimate rather than the ultimate dimension of the Christian message. But this does not render the penultimate insignificant. To preach justification by grace and nothing about the moral life that must follow leads to the strange condition among Christians, as Helmut Thielicke once so wonderfully described it, of "the devout heart gripped by God's grace, but not yet pumping blood to the extremities of the body." The result is a kind of moral "numbness in the extremities," demonstrated by an unholy dichotomy between heart and hands, doctrine and life, church and world.[27] That moral numbness, in turn, is not only unfaithful to Jesus our Lord but also can have quite specific and devastating consequences of its own in the societies in which we live. Thielicke mentions the perpetration of the Holocaust in his land, Germany, a land full of supposedly "saved by grace" Christians. Perhaps we can think of a few moral problems we ourselves face as a nation.

In this chapter we have outlined a distressing problem and have sought to make sense of why it exists. In the next we will move to a constructive proposal concerning how preachers can reenvision the moral dimension of the gospel and thus of the ministry of proclamation.

NOTES

1. David Buttrick, "Up Against the Powers That Be," in Thomas G. Long and Cornelius Plantinga Jr., eds., *A Chorus of Witnesses* (Grand Rapids: Eerdmans, 1994), 223.

2. Ronald J. Allen, "What We Are Really Preaching: A Report on Empirical Studies of Preaching," *Pulpit Digest* 78 (September/October 1997), 83.

3. This literature includes such works as Jesse Jai McNeil, *The Preacher-Prophet in Mass Society,* rev. ed. (Nashville: Townsend, 1993). See also James H. Harris, *Preaching Liberation* (Minneapolis: Augsburg Fortress, 1995); J. Alfred Smith Sr., *Outstanding Black Sermons* (Valley Forge, Pa.: Judson, 1976); Kelly Miller Smith, *Social Crisis Preaching* (Atlanta: Mercer, 1984).

4. Frederick Buechner, *Telling the Truth* (New York: HarperCollins, 1977), 18.

5. See especially McNeil, *The Preacher-Prophet in Mass Society,* a title that reveals the author's perspective on the matter.

6. An exception is Elizabeth Achtemeier's fine exposition of Genesis 3 in "The Story of Us All: A Christian Exposition of Genesis 3," in *Preaching Biblical Texts,* ed. Fredrick C. Holmgren and Herman E. Schaalman (Grand Rapids: Eerdmans, 1995), 1–10.

7. Martin Luther King Jr., "Letter from Birmingham City Jail," in James M. Washington, ed., *A Testament of Hope: The Essential Writings of Martin Luther King, Jr.* (New York: Harper and Row, 1986), 298–99.

8. Exceptions include Stan L. LeQuire, ed., *The Best Preaching on Earth* (Valley Forge, Pa.: Judson, 1996); Elizabeth Achtemeier, *Nature, God, and Pulpit* (Grand Rapids: Eerdmans, 1992); Dieter Hessel, ed., *For Creation's Sake* (Philadelphia: Geneva, 1985).

9. J. Alfred Smith, "Preaching and Social Concerns," in Michael Duduit, ed., *A Handbook of Contemporary Preaching* (Nashville: Broadman & Holman, 1992), 508.

10. Ibid., 508–9.

11. Bryan Chapell, *Christ-Centered Preaching* (Grand Rapids: Baker, 1994), 12.

12. Smith, "Preaching and Social Concerns," 509.

13. McNeil, *Preacher-Prophet in Mass Society,* 42.

14. Smith, *Social Crisis Preaching,* 36–37.

15. One homiletician who shares this concern about seminary training in preaching is Clyde E. Fant. See his *Preaching for Today,* rev. ed. (San Francisco: HarperCollins, 1987), preface.

16. Quoted in Helmut Thielicke, *The Trouble with the Church* (Grand Rapids: Baker, 1965), 81.

17. Quoted in John Maxwell, "Relationships: A New Beginning or a Bitter End," (audio tape) *INJOY Life Club* 12, no. 10 (April 1997).

18. *Western Recorder* (October 7, 1997), 8.

19. Thielicke, *The Trouble with the Church*, 112.

20. Karl Barth, *The Preaching of the Gospel* (Philadelphia: Westminster, 1963), 75–76. See also McNeil, *Preacher-Prophet in Mass Society,* especially 79–80, and Harris, *Preaching Liberation,* viii and *passim.*

21. A recent evangelical classic that attempts to dismantle this misunderstanding of the gospel message is Dallas Willard, *The Spirit of the Disciplines* (New York: HarperCollins, 1988).

22. Arthur Van Seters, "Introduction: Widening Our Vision," in Arthur Van Seters, ed., *Preaching as a Social Act: Theology and Practice* (Nashville: Abingdon, 1988), 20.

23. James Carroll and John Carroll, *Preaching the Hard Sayings of Jesus* (Peabody, Mass.: Hendrickson, 1996), 65.

24. Barth, *Preaching of the Gospel,* 42.

25. Buechner, *Telling the Truth*, 18–19, 35–36.

26. Dietrich Bonhoeffer, *Ethics* (New York: Macmillan, 1955), 125; cf. 120–43.

27. Thielicke, *The Trouble with the Church,* 10–12.

CHAPTER TWO

A Fresh Start

Reenvisioning the Moral Dimension
of Christian Preaching

There are as many ways of characterizing Christian morality as
there are of describing Christian preaching. Just as no single
approach to preaching should be viewed as the final and authoritative word on the subject, no approach to Christian morality
deserves such lofty standing. Likewise, then, our effort in this
chapter to offer "ethics for preaching" comes to the reader with
all appropriate humility. We are not saying the final word on
the subject; but as we review the literature, it appears we are
among the few to say a word about it at all. We hope that others
will join the conversation.

Here we offer a synopsis of the moral dimension of Christian preaching as we see it. Our goal is to lay out a kind of
moral grid for the congregational preacher's use, beginning
with some reflections on the moral dimension of Scripture.
We assume that many preachers already have developed similar
grids for other dimensions of preaching, such as the doctrinal and the pastoral. But if our literature review and church
experience can be trusted, this grid is less likely to have
been developed for the moral dimension of Christian proclamation. Our fond hope is that this model can be instructive
in reenvisioning that dimension and in thereby enhancing the
preaching ministry.

The Moral Dimension of Scripture

The place to begin is with the preacher's textbook, the Bible. The Bible is filled with moral content – that is, material relevant to the church's Spirit-empowered effort to know and to do God's will and to advance God's kingdom. We have already argued that much of the time the moral dimension of the biblical message is truncated or overlooked. Perhaps a "moral dimension walking tour" through the Scriptures is in order as the first part of this discussion, with hints along the way concerning the use of various genres of Scripture for preaching.[1]

Moral Commands

Everyone recognizes that one aspect of the moral dimension of Scripture is its body of direct and explicit moral commands. The Bible certainly contains numerous examples of such rules or commands, many of which are burned into Christian consciousness: "If someone strikes you on the right cheek, turn to him the other also" (Matthew 5:39); "Love your neighbor as yourself" (Matthew 22:39); "You shall not murder" (Exodus 20:13). Others, of course, are more obscure and sometimes quite difficult: "Anyone who curses his father or mother must be put to death" (Exodus 21:17). "If a thief is caught breaking in and is struck so that he dies, the defender is not guilty of bloodshed" (Exodus 22:2). "Women should remain silent in the churches" (1 Corinthians 14:34). Note that some moral instructions offer positive commands while others are negative in form. Likewise, some establish general rules or principles (apodictic commands) while others seek to employ these standards in particular cases (casuistic applications). Some moral commands focus on outward actions while others address inward attitudes or motivations. The most concentrated form of direct moral instruction is found in Old Testament legal materials (woven into the books Exodus through Deuteronomy), which include commands related to a bewildering range of ritual, cultic, dietary, moral, and social concerns and were originally intended to govern the total life of ancient Israel.

How exactly that material applies to Christians has always

been a matter of considerable debate in the church and is an important issue for preaching. Some preachers ignore Old Testament law altogether as if it has no continuing usefulness for Christian moral instruction. A handful of preachers, on the other hand, draw on Old Testament law in a rigid and legalistic fashion. The best approach, we believe, is to draw distinctions between the materials one finds in Old Testament law. Texts such as the Ten Commandments, the love command in Leviticus, and the call to love God with all your heart (Deuteronomy 6:5) clearly are of abiding significance for the church. Others – particularly cultic, dietary, and ritual purity regulations – do not apply directly to the church. However, even with such texts, one normally can extract principles useful in Christian moral instruction.[2] Given the Bible's own insistence that "all Scripture is...useful for teaching" (2 Timothy 3:16), it is incumbent upon the preacher to seek out ways to do just that.

Direct moral exhortation, of course, can be found scattered in most other genres of Scripture as well, most significantly in the teachings of Jesus, such as the Sermon on the Mount, the most important single body of moral teaching from Jesus that we have. To what extent the teachings of Jesus or others should be understood as commands or as "lawlike" in character is also a matter of perennial debate. We understand the teachings of Jesus to be authoritative for his followers; he intended for us to live according to his words. However, they do not function as law insofar as law breaking or law keeping might be understood as disqualifying or qualifying one for eternal salvation. Instead, Jesus' teachings are grounded in God's grace and intended to enable us to live out God's will and to advance God's kingdom. For this reason, they should be studied closely and preached regularly. In our view, the actual preaching and teaching of Jesus plays far too small a part in most contemporary Christian proclamation. Congregations need a steady diet of Jesus' teachings if they are to be healthy.

Likewise, direct moral instruction characterizes the thunderous proclamations of the Old Testament prophets. The prophets, while they must not be understood as constituting the entirety of the moral dimension of Scripture, are indeed an important part of it.[3] Tragically, some popular preaching makes use of the prophets solely as soothsayers of the end times; yet that was not their intent and is a terrible misappropriation. The Old Testament prophets are best understood in their original context as reminding Israel of the meaning of the covenant relationship God graciously established with them and of the necessity of abiding by its terms. The prophets hold Israel accountable for obedience to the Law – primarily emphasizing its moral and social aspects rather than its cultic dimension (Isaiah 1:11-17), focus attention on the needs of the most vulnerable in the land (Isaiah 1:23; Jeremiah 22:13-17), and demand that inner purity of heart and motive accompany any effort to demonstrate or attain outer purity through worship practices (Hosea 6:6; Micah 6:6-8). Their words speak both to the specifics of their own context and to the realities of any context. They are a critical component of the moral dimension of preaching yet are profoundly neglected in most churches. This is one reason why, as Kelly Miller Smith has put it, so many pulpits offer merely an "echo" of existing social arrangements rather than a cry for social transformation.[4]

Moral Narratives

Moral commands and direct exhortations are an important part of the Bible's moral witness, but they do not exhaust it. Christian preaching must plumb the moral dimension of other types of biblical materials. Consider the numerous biblical narratives, like the patriarchal history in Genesis 12-50, the accounts of the judges and kings in the historical books of the Old Testament, the gospel accounts of Jesus' ministry, or the story of the rise of the early church in the book of Acts. We hardly need to be reminded of the profound impact of the stories we find therein – stories such as those concerning Jacob and Esau (Genesis 27-33), Joseph and his brothers (Genesis 37-50), Samson and Delilah (Judges 13-16), David and Bathsheba (2 Samuel 11), Absalom (2 Samuel 15-19), Ananias and Sapphira (Acts 5), and Stephen (Acts 7). These teach us morally even when the texts themselves never explicitly draw a moral lesson. Other biblical narratives are invented explicitly for instructional purposes, such as Nathan's parable of the ewe lamb

(2 Samuel 12) or Jesus' story of the Good Samaritan (Luke 10).
Indeed, it is possible and probably best to view the parables as
their own unique genre of moral instruction. Frequently, Christians experience moral challenge through character studies of
the lives of biblical exemplars, such as David, Moses, or Paul,
or of course, Jesus. Also instructive is examination of accounts
of moral failure, such as Peter's betrayal of Jesus and its after-
math (Matthew 26), Rehoboam's foolish decisions as a young
king (1 Kings 12), the demise of Saul (1 Samuel 18ff.) or, more
subtly, Solomon (1 Kings 11), or the character and decisions
of Pilate (Matthew 27). The use of such narratives in preaching
has a long history; yet many have observed that in our own non-
linear, nonpropositional, experience-oriented, postmodern age,
narratives are particularly well suited for the communication of
biblical truth.

In a broader sense, the biblical message as a whole takes
the form of a narrative, bracketed on the front end by the
Garden of Eden of Genesis and on the back end by the New
Jerusalem of Revelation. Lewis Smedes has talked about the
way Scripture offers Christians a "panoramic vision of life as
a whole," a frame of reference within which Christians are
to situate themselves and understand the meaning and purpose of their lives.[5] At its heart this is a narrative about God's
character, actions, intentions, and will. Yet it is also a narrative about humanity generally, about those human beings and
groups engaged in covenantal relationship with God, and even
about the nonhuman inhabitants of the created order. The very
theological categories we often take for granted – creation, fall,
redemption, eschatological consummation – reflect the plot of
the master biblical narrative as it unfolds in Scripture.

Some have argued that it is precisely this narrative that is the
most significant or possibly even the only morally relevant dimension of Scripture.[6] We think this overstates the case and
agree with Tom Long when he writes, "Despite the value of
claiming that the gospel is essentially narrative and that every
scriptural text fits somehow into the overarching biblical story,
the fact of the matter is that there are non-narrative texts, and
for good reason. The biblical writers do not always tell stories."[7]
Yet it is also true that the nonnarrative texts – we think here

of the nonnarrative moral instruction texts – make sense only within a coherent vision of the overall biblical story. Too often this broader vision is lost, and the moral dimension of preaching devolves into a series of disconnected and uninterpreted moral exhortations or commands. For that matter, the particular "microstories" of Scripture must be connected to the broader "macro-Story" that characterizes the Bible as a whole. Too frequently, especially in the moral instruction of children, this connection is not made. The preacher skillful in plumbing the depths of Scripture's moral dimension will be able to connect particular teachings and particular stories with the panoramic story offered by Scripture as a whole.

Proverbs

Scriptural moral teaching sometimes comes in the form of moral aphorisms or proverbs, most commonly in the Wisdom literature of the Old Testament, but also in the distinctly wisdom-type sayings of Jesus. Many generations of believers have found practical moral instruction through the book of Proverbs, much of which, interestingly enough, is not framed in terms of direct moral instruction at all. Instead, moral observations are made, drawn from all manner of human and even animal experience, from which the reader is implicitly invited to draw the obvious conclusion. "All hard work brings a profit, but mere talk leads only to poverty" (Proverbs 14:23). *Therefore, work hard;* yet the text does not say this. The book of Ecclesiastes, though rightly interpreted as a critical interaction with the Wisdom tradition, also contains some Wisdom-type moral instruction: "The quiet words of the wise are more to be heeded than the shouts of a ruler of fools" (9:17). Job, meanwhile, is a rich mix of narrative, anguished and increasingly angry dialogue, poetry, and much more, all probing the Wisdom tradition's truism that the good prosper and the wicked suffer. Job 31 offers one of the richest depictions of moral integrity to be found anywhere in Scripture (see sermon 6).

Preaching on these biblical materials carries both opportunities and risks. On the positive side, the exceedingly practical and experiential nature of most scriptural proverbs makes them readily accessible to the average listener. Their emphasis on the ingredients of success or disaster in life translates remarkably well across the chasm between their original context and our own. They are particularly helpful, we find, in communicating moral truth to young people, who particularly enjoy the proverbs' clever and picturesque language. Risks associated with preaching from the Proverbs are of two basic types. First, because the Wisdom tradition generally links success with right living and disaster with foolish conduct, it is possible to extract from these texts a theology that uniformly blames people for all that goes wrong in their lives. Both the book of Job and the teachings of Jesus are necessary to counteract this tendency. Even more importantly, the Proverbs can be preached in a manner that promotes works righteousness and legalism. They are a helpful guide in the context of a strong overall theology of salvation and the Christian life, and should not be preached apart from such a theology.

Apostolic Instruction

In the New Testament epistles we find another genre of morally significant material. In these books we overhear the moral instruction of one or another apostle – mainly Paul – to a particular body of Christian believers or sometimes to a broader group of congregations. Preaching on the apostolic epistles requires use of some of the same principles we discussed related to the use of Old Testament law. It is important to draw a distinction between moral instructions and exhortations that are best viewed as abiding and universally applicable and those texts that are more specific, temporary, and context bound. Even in the latter case, it is important to seek to extract from such texts those principles that do translate, at least by analogy, into our contemporary context. Paul's instruction related to eating meat sacrificed to idols (1 Corinthians 8) makes a helpful illustration. We do not currently face that particular problem, and thus the passage on its face is of no direct applicability. However, it is possible – indeed, imperative – to find within that passage a key principle related to life in Christian community: Christians have considerable liberty in certain areas of conduct, but their liberty must always be constrained by their love. When in doubt, liberty yields to love. This principle is of great significance; one can think of many contemporary applications.

While the church has been nourished by these texts for the whole of its history, the unique characteristics of this genre require that the application of these instructions to ourselves be undertaken with care, lest we confuse context-specific moral instructions with those more appropriately interpreted as being of abiding and direct application to the church.

Prayers

The Psalms are other portions of Scripture that have a moral dimension. These are hymn-prayers and very rarely contain direct moral instruction. Yet immersion in the Psalms has a profound impact on readers, not by telling us what to do but by showing us what to be – by modeling how to pray. Consider the impact of the penitential psalm par excellence, Psalm 51, in teaching us the stance of honesty with self and God, repentance, contrition, humility, and trust in God's mercy. This reminds us that the Scriptures *form* our character at least as much as they *inform* our moral decision making. That dimension of the biblical message needs to be preached intentionally.

Another important contribution of the Psalms is in the dimensions of nurture and comfort they offer to our congregations. Arthur Van Seters, making reference to a paper by Bonnie Benda, has wisely argued that as preachers we must "start *with* the congregation, not *against* it."[8] Though there are times in which confrontation is required, the moral dimension of preaching should not be generally conceived as "a radical, condemning voice standing over and above the congregation thundering against the evils of society."[9] Quite to the contrary, there are times in which our congregation or one of its members might be the victim of social injustice; here we offer words of comfort, nurture, and concern. Similarly, there ought to be times in which moral progress has been made in our midst, and our best response is affirmation and celebration. It is *together*, as the body of Christ, preacher and congregation alike and in the same boat, that we seek to grow to maturity. The Psalms can perhaps help us remember that this is the case.

Apocalyptic

Another example of moral insight that can be found in unexpected places is in that genre of literature most commonly called apocalyptic (large sections of Ezekiel, parts of Daniel and Zechariah, the apocalyptic sections of the Synoptic Gospels, and Revelation). These esoteric, imaginative, and frequently very difficult to interpret materials largely focus on the mysterious events of the end of time. They provide abundant fodder for end-times speculation, which has made many writers of dubious quality quite handsomely rich. But what is less frequently noted is the moral stance engendered by biblical apocalyptic. "Be careful, or your hearts will be weighed down with dissipation, drunkenness and the anxieties of life, and that day will close on you unexpectedly like a trap" (Luke 21:34). These were Christ's words near the close of his discourse on the end of the age, as recorded by Luke. Note that earnest expectation of that awesome "Day" is to create a stance of moral watchfulness, sobriety, and focus on what matters most. What we have here is eschatologically grounded moral vigilance. Paul's epistles often are redolent with the same theme and spirit, and it is a stance that has characterized many of the great saints of the church to this day.

Contemporary preachers face the significant challenge of rescuing the apocalyptic portions of Scripture from abuse and reacquainting their congregations with the true moral significance of these materials. It is especially important to attack the moral quietism and complacency that so frequently are created by pop apocalyptic speculations. If the world is going to end by a certain date and human history, by God's design, is spiraling downward, why bother to undertake any moral effort at all? This disastrous way of reading the apocalyptic portions of Scripture must be named and rejected.

Let us summarize what we have said thus far. The first task for the preacher is to become acquainted or reacquainted with the full range of moral content that can be found in the Scripture and then simply to exposit the texts faithfully as they stand. From Genesis to Revelation, from narrative to law, all Scripture contains a moral dimension. Seeing it may involve a kind of reorientation process as one learns to recognize the rich moral content that has been blocked from one's vision.

Bible, Ethics, and Preaching: Difficult Issues

Still, it is not quite as easy as this. Many difficult questions emerge at the intersection of Scripture and Christian morality, such as: What principle of selection determines which aspects, themes, sections, or genres of Scripture will move to the center of attention in moral instruction in the church? How does one discover and justify this principle of selection? When reading Scripture for moral content, what types of moral norms are we mainly seeking to find? Are we looking for laws, rules, principles, guidelines, proverbs, or perhaps virtues, practices, visions, or broad theological/moral orientations? How shall Scripture help us deal with contemporary moral issues, such as genetic engineering, not addressed by Scripture at all? How shall Old and New Testament moral instruction be related to each other? Does Old Testament law still apply to the church? If so, how? Who is understood to be the primary recipient of the Bible's moral instruction – the individual human being, the society, the human family, the Christian congregation, or someone else? Finally, is it possible, and should we even try, to organize this diverse array of morally significant biblical material into a coherent whole? Is there some fundamental motif or theme around which we should organize the moral dimension of our preaching?

These are important and much discussed questions in theology and ethics. The answers to such questions vary widely in different confessional traditions within the church, and most are a matter of considerable debate in contemporary academic and church circles. All we can offer here is a brief sketch of our own approach; but we do think that these issues need to be addressed by everyone whose task it is to offer moral instruction to the people of God. At the very least, a "rough and ready" working practical theology/ethic is needed if one's moral teaching and handling of the Scripture for ethics is going to exhibit any kind of coherence.

In our approach, the place to begin is by affirming the centrality of Jesus Christ for the use of Scripture in preaching on ethical matters as on all other issues and concerns. Jesus must be central, not only understood theologically in terms of his incarnation, atoning death for sin, and resurrection, but also in the terms of the details of his life, ministry, and teaching.[10]

This means that our proclamation of the moral teaching of the Scripture should be refracted through the lens of Jesus' own moral teaching, including his approach to and use of Scripture. We should imitate him on this as on every other point. Thus, because Jesus clearly had a very high view of the authority of Scripture for the moral life, attacking those who ignored, did away with, or "relaxed" the commandments (Matthew 5:19), so we too should proclaim that Scripture is the authoritative guide for life and was written to be obeyed and practiced. Further, Jesus demonstrated his familiarity with, respect for, and submission to the entire canonical witness of his Bible, which we call the Old Testament, and we should do the same. We should mine the whole canon for Christian ethical proclamation, as we have already sought to demonstrate. The Old Testament should not, at least in our view, primarily be presented as moral law for the church but should be presented as offering authoritative instruction. The key is to read Old Testament Scripture in the way Jesus did – through a prophetic interpretive grid. That grid emphasized the Old Testament's moral aspects rather than its cultic dimension, its focus on the least of these, its demand for purity of heart as well as performance of deeds, and its vision of the sovereign God and the coming of the kingdom.

At least as important as the foregoing is the importance of placing the moral teaching of Jesus himself at the very center of the use of Scripture for ethical preaching. It is surprising how frequently the moral teaching (and moral example) of the Son of God and Savior of the world are ignored as Christians debate the moral issues of the day. Christians – including preachers – unfortunately do not always seem to know what to do with the teachings of their own Savior. We must simultaneously affirm the usefulness and authority of all Scripture and Jesus Christ as the lens through which the canon is to be viewed. The Bible should not be seen as a flat document; Jesus Christ is its peak and its very center. No moral issue should be addressed apart from careful consideration of the meaning of Jesus Christ for reflection on that issue. Sometimes this will involve analysis of specific moral teachings uttered by Jesus that directly bear on contemporary moral issues; other times such teachings will be unavailable, yet other dimensions of Jesus' person and work will always be relevant and must be central.

Thus, exposition of Jesus' moral teachings must be a regular part of the preacher's repertoire. Meanwhile, topical discussions of contemporary issues, when they occur, must never stray far from Jesus, even when no explicit words from him on these issues exist. As the rest of the canon is examined for morally focused preaching, texts should be brought to the people of God only after being considered during the preparation process in light of Jesus Christ. Thus, we find the principle of selection, the fundamental motif around which the moral dimension of our preaching can be organized: Jesus.

We raised certain difficult issues at the beginning of this section that we have yet to resolve. We now turn to these under the rubric of constructing a grid for the moral dimension of preaching.

The Moral Dimension of Preaching: A Grid

The content of preaching is ultimately indistinguishable from the content of the Christian faith and the biblical message. As many interpreters of preaching have suggested, the preacher is essentially a practical theologian, bringing the Word of God as he or she understands it to the people of God. As anybody who preaches every week knows, this is a fearsome responsibility. It is difficult enough to interpret rightly for oneself that entire body of canonical writings known as the Scriptures and that entire body of historical teaching known as Christian theology that has developed over two millennia. But then to bring that body of Scripture and theology to bear in comprehensible, practical, and meaningful ways to the people in the pew each week – while managing myriad other responsibilities of local church life – poses an even more difficult challenge.

One dimension of that task is our focus here: that dimension of practical theology known as Christian ethics. Here again there is a vast body of relevant Scripture and two millennia of relevant tradition and teaching – not to mention the omnipresent and ever-multiplying moral challenges that emerge from contemporary personal and social life.

So the preacher needs some help. The grid we are about to offer distills some of the most significant insights and arguments in recent years in the field of Christian ethics for the use of the preacher. This model can be used as a kind of checklist in assessing the adequacy and thoroughness of one's treatment of the moral dimension of Scripture and of the Christian message.

Four Kinds of Moral Norms

Christian ethicists debate many things, but perhaps the most basic question is the following: *What kinds of moral norms exist in Scripture and should exist in Christian moral reasoning?* We named this question earlier when first listing the difficult issues that arise at the intersection of Scripture and ethics. It is one of those foundational questions that few people think about in the normal course of daily events. Yet we cannot even begin to understand the content of Christian morality until we understand its form. And we need clarity on this issue to be prepared for adequate preaching on the moral dimension of the gospel.

In the literature of Christian ethics, four kinds (or levels) of moral norms are frequently discussed: *particular judgments, rules, principles,* and *ground-of-meaning claims.* Human beings organize and communicate their moral convictions at each of these four levels. While it is possible to hear all of these levels employed by one person at different times, most people tend to key in on one level or another as the heart of their way of thinking and talking about morality. Meanwhile, people who think about morality for a living – ethicists – have generated an array of arguments to support a focus on one level or another as the heart of biblical and/or Christian morality. It is our argument here that Scripture communicates moral truth at each of these levels – our walking tour through Scripture indicated as much – and thus it is wrong to choose one or another as the only legitimate kind of moral norm. Yet we will argue that the ground-of-meaning level, which we will call the "theological framework" level, is the starting point for all moral norms and is thus ultimately the most significant kind of moral norm. But first we need to sketch what we mean by each kind of norm.

Particular judgments are those moral evaluations that have to do with one particular case or situation. "It was wrong of Judas to betray Jesus" is an example of a particular moral judgment. "Sally should not have divorced Sam" is another. The key characteristic of a particular judgment is that the moral judgment as articulated applies to one particular case only. Scripture contains numerous examples of particular judgments in single cases, such as Nathan's judgment of the wrongness of David's actions related to Bathsheba and Uriah (2 Samuel 12), or John the Baptist's condemnation of Herod and Herodias (Matthew 14:1–12). Likewise, people make particular judgments every day about both the character and actions of others.

A second kind of moral norm is a rule. Rules are different from particular judgments in many ways. Rules apply not just to one particular case, but to all similar cases. Indeed, rules are designed to tell us directly and concretely what to do or not to do in particular cases. Rules in everyday life come in a variety of forms, such as laws, terms of employment, and regulations governing sporting activities. Likewise, in Scripture rules also take a variety of forms, the most familiar of which are divine commands, as discussed above. Many people understand morality solely at the rule level and read the Scripture in that way. We have already alluded to the significant presence of rules in Scripture, but we think it is a mistake to understand the Bible's moral witness solely at this level.

It is easy to see that rules mark a step back from the specificity of particular judgments, because they apply not just to one situation but to all relevantly similar situations. The third kind of moral norm, principles, moves to an even broader and more general level. Principles are one level deeper than rules. They do not tell us directly what to do or not to do. Instead, they provide the basis for rules, which do just that. The principle supports the rule, and the rule spells out a direct application of the principle. Likewise, principles provide a basis for criticizing rules.

In Scripture, a key principle is neighbor love. That principle is taught again and again throughout the canon and is a major focus of Jesus' teachings. One can think of a variety of scriptural rules that function as direct applications of the principle of neighbor love; for example, "Don't show favoritism" (James 2:1). This rule does not just hang out in scriptural space for no reason, but instead exists because of the broader principle of neighbor love upon which it is grounded.

Now the problem is that sometimes a rule gets disconnected from the principle that is its foundation. The rule "Don't show favoritism," for example, might be taken to mean that no steps of any type may be taken to open doors of employment to whose who have had less educational and economic opportunity than others have had. The contemporary debate over various forms of affirmative action comes to mind. Or, for example, parents might foolishly decide that it is wrong to treat any of their children differently from any other, even if one of them is younger or has a disability. The principle of neighbor love, which grounds the rule "Don't show favoritism," also critiques any understanding or application of the rule, which itself violates that principle, as in this case.

The final kind of moral norm can be found at the ground-of-meaning level. The best entry point to an understanding of this level is to consider this scenario. Suppose someone asks you why you are committed to the principle of neighbor love, as outlined above. As a Christian, you are most likely to say something like, "Because God commands it in the Bible." Or, "Because Jesus taught it." Or, "Because I want to be like Jesus." Suppose then that you are asked, "Why do you care what God or Jesus commands, and why do you want to be like Jesus?" The only answer you can give is something like: "I have given my life to Christ. It is my ultimate commitment. I don't base it on

anything else. I base it on God." At this point, further question-
ing would be fruitless. The questioner, and you, have reached
the very rock-bottom level, the ultimate grounding for Christian
ethics. No further digging is possible. First there are particular judgments; underneath these are rules; underneath rules are
principles; and underneath principles, at least for believers, are
the character, actions, and will of God. Because you cannot dig
any deeper than this, ultimately the ground-of-meaning level is
the most important.

Now, we hope, it is clear why we have taken you on this
excursion into technical ethics talk related to moral norms.
We think that the moral dimension of preaching becomes adequate when it moves in appropriate ways up and down these
four moral norm levels. The moral dimension of preaching is
handled well when its "house" is built in the following way:

1. Its foundation is a biblically sound overall theological framework.

2. Its first floor, building upon this foundation, is a clearly articulated set of key moral principles.

3. Its second floor is a set of particular rules related to the living of
   life that are adequately grounded in the principles just below it.

4. Its third floor consists of particular moral judgments made from
   the pulpit concerning the issues facing a particular people of
   God in a particular time and place.

This house metaphor is helpful in illuminating the significance of rightly ordering each kind of moral norm. It is
absolutely critical that particular judgments be grounded in
rules, rules grounded in broader principles, and principles
grounded in an adequate understanding of the character and
will of God. We will say more about this as we unfold this grid
in more detail in the next section.

At the Core: The Theological Framework

Preaching is fundamentally a theological task, as Tom Long
and Ed Farley, along with others, have reminded us.[11] This is
a claim we do not dispute even in this most ethics-minded of
preaching textbooks. Indeed, as our model indicates, we believe that ethical instruction from the pulpit must be grounded

in foundational theological convictions. Otherwise, the moral dimension of preaching thins out into an unhelpful and misleading moralism.

When we speak of the theological foundation for the moral dimension of preaching, at least two issues come immediately to the surface. On the one hand, we must consider the *form* in which theological convictions should be presented. On the other, we need to reflect on the *content* of this theological material.

On the issue of form, at least two major alternatives can be sketched. One approach to theology, especially as it relates to preaching, is to offer propositional doctrinal formulations. Thus, the theological framework for preaching consists of doctrines of God, humanity, Christ, salvation, the church, eschatology, and so on. On this approach, the moral dimension of preaching would primarily consist of deriving moral norms from systematic doctrinal truths and/or developing a doctrinal approach to the Christian moral life, and then presenting this material from the pulpit accordingly. Thus, the doctrine of Creation, for example, contains certain moral implications, and as these are unfolded, one witnesses the moral dimension of preaching.[12] Or, alternatively, there is the doctrine of sanctification, and the explication of this doctrine is viewed as the explication of the moral dimension of the gospel.

An entirely different approach to the form of theology can be found in the renewed emphasis on narrative. Here, as we indicated earlier, the message of the Bible is understood primarily in the form of story – both one master Story and the hundreds of particular stories that are a part of the broader biblical narrative. The same ground is covered as in the systematic/doctrinal approach: creation, sin, redemption, eschatology, and so on. However, it is covered not by abstracting doctrine from the biblical story but instead simply by telling the story itself. The moral dimension of preaching, then, develops within the framework of the broader biblical story.

Thomas Troeger has made a strong case for the particular value, not only of narrative, but of metaphors, symbols, and "myth," in preaching. He argues that at the deepest wellsprings of human behavior and human consciousness one finds precisely such symbols, myths, dreams, narratives, and visions, rather than, for example, rational arguments or crisp doctrinal propositions. Comparing the impact for evil of Adolf Hitler, and the impact for good of Martin Luther King Jr., Troeger traces the effectiveness of both to their ability to reach the mythic-poetic level of human consciousness. The lessons for preaching are clear: "Anyone, then, who is going to preach on social issues needs to understand the power of myth and its poetic language of image and symbol, their grip upon the landscape of the heart, and the enormous energies that they may release for good or evil."[13]

While there are many who would go to the mat defending one or the other of these two approaches – propositional or narrative – we think that for the purposes of the moral dimension of preaching each has its place. Both are different ways of organizing the same biblical content, different lenses for viewing the same scene, and they speak to different dimensions of the human person. What we do know to be unacceptable is to attempt to undertake the moral – or any other – dimension of preaching without offering some kind of coherent biblical theological framework as its fundamental ground.

Of course, it is not enough to settle on some theological form. The content of the theology that grounds the moral dimension of preaching is surely of even greater significance. We are not telling the reader anything shocking when we say that the biblical Story (or biblical "doctrine") has been construed in a wild variety of ways. The combination of a closed canon and an open religious imagination has proven to be fertile ground for an endless set of permutations of Christian theology, some of them with quite destructive moral implications. The literature of preaching clearly reflects much of this diversity. Essentially, one finds in that literature echoes of whatever theological debates were raging in the broader academic/ecclesial world at the time. We do not need to rehearse those discussions, but we would like to indicate one key issue relevant to our task.

That issue is the use of a central theological motif as the organizing principle for preaching. For example, in James H. Harris's book *Preaching Liberation*, he defines liberation preaching as "preaching in the context of oppression with a view toward liberation."[14] There is little question in that work that the theological motif of liberation is viewed normatively as central to the entire preaching enterprise. The same is true of Kelly Miller Smith's book *Social Crisis Preaching.* [15] More broadly, liberation functions as a critical theological motif in much of the preaching literature that emerges from the black church tradition as well as from Two-Thirds World liberation theologians.[16]

While we believe the theme of liberation is indisputably biblical and is neglected by the more comfortable white church, we are suspicious of the elevation of any single theological motif to a central position in either theology or preaching. The moral dimension of preaching is best served by a broad theological foundation that makes room for all significant biblical themes, motifs, doctrines, and narratives. Preachers should read widely both in Scripture and in theology to continually refresh and broaden their theological thinking. For breadth of theological vision, we like the older formation of the black Baptist preacher-scholar Jesse Jai McNeil:

> When what the preacher-prophet says voices the characteristics and essential ideas of the Bible, he is an authentic spokesman for God. These ideas will include the creative power, sovereignty, righteousness and holiness of God; the creatureliness and sinfulness of man, God's judgment upon sin, and the redemption of men from sin though Jesus Christ; God's love of man as his heavenly Father and man's love of man as his earthly brother; a community of justice and order and freedom on earth, and eternal life with God in the world to come.[17]

Even this fine formulation misses such theological essentials as the nature and character of the church, God as Trinity, and the role of the Holy Spirit in Christian living. The best approach is to match aspects of a broadly understood biblical theology with the seasons of a congregation's life and a discerning reading of the "signs of the times" in society and world. This will help the preacher to avoid narrowing his or her focus too sharply by becoming fixated on a signal point of biblical revelation. The goal is a broad and well-balanced understanding of the character, actions, and will of God.

The First Floor: Principles

Some ethicists and theologians have suggested that the theological ground-of-meaning level is all we really need. Whether understood doctrinally or in narrative fashion, central theological convictions essentially speak for themselves, at least to the discerning Christian individual or faith community. God is loving, so we must be loving; that settles the matter. The Samaritan did the right thing; go and do likewise. So it is argued.

While we have already contended that the theological foundation for ethical preaching is the most fundamental, it cannot be left on its own. The particular beliefs, behaviors, loyalties, and virtues that these convictions generate must be spelled out in the form of principles, and sometimes rules, even at times in very concrete particular judgments, in order to give clear direction to the church. These rules and principles make clear what we understand the implications of the gospel story to be, concretely and specifically. Otherwise, we fail to give definite ethical direction to our people, a problem all too characteristic of the North American church in many sectors today, and with disastrous consequences.

The first place to begin to translate theological convictions into moral teaching is at the level of moral principle. Principles, as we have already indicated, are broad statements of moral conviction that undergird both rules and particular moral judgments, and are themselves grounded in foundational theological beliefs. One way to distinguish a principle from a rule is this: Principles do not tell one directly and concretely what to do or not to do, but provide the underlying basis for many rules that do exactly that. Thus, Jesus' command that we love our neighbors functions as a moral principle; it does not tell us exactly what to do. But it does generate and undergird particular scriptural rules, such as "feed the hungry" and "don't show favoritism."

Preachers need to think through the scriptural witness in terms of its foundational moral principles and then weave these principles regularly into their preaching. Our own view is that several central scriptural moral principles need to be lifted up for particular attention. These include neighbor love, justice, the sacredness of human life, holiness, truthfulness, and fidelity to covenant. Each of these principles – though this list is not exhaustive – receives considerable attention in the Scripture, and each is spelled out in terms of dozens of particular moral rules, both in their positive and negative formulations:

Principle	*Rule*
neighbor love	do not retaliate; forgive one another
justice	do not take bribes; act on behalf of the stranger
sacredness of life	do not murder; defend the innocent
holiness	do not commit fornication; purify your thoughts of lust
truthfulness	do not bear false witness; let your yes be yes
fidelity to covenant	do not commit adultery; guard your heart

As we noted earlier, one value of principles is the check they impose on our rule making. If, for example, we were to preach that all congregants must wear only seventeenth-century clothing, we could be challenged to ground that rule in a relevant principle. If we were to respond that the key principle is holiness, then we could be challenged once more to demonstrate how the rule fits with the principle. Or, alternatively, we could be challenged to consider the import of the principle of our freedom in Christ (1 Corinthians 8) as it pertains to the matter. This reminds us that frequently it is not one principle but several that are relevant to the moral life and to particular moral situations. At times, these principles can conflict, and thus we must choose between them. The Bible teaches that the principle of love stands at the top of the moral hierarchy when decisions between principles must be made (Matthew 22:34–40). In any case, conflicting principles drive us back to *their* foundation: the character, conduct, and will of God and the theological framework we discussed above.

As with the theological framework level, some ethicists have argued that the fundamental level of moral norms is the level of principle. The Southern Baptist ethicist Henlee Barnette, whose career spanned the 1950s to 1980s, coined the term *principlism* to describe this stance, which he embraced. He argued that a handful of broad principles are more fundamental and function more adequately than dozens of rules for the moral life. Like many ethicists of his generation, particularly in the mainline and postfundamentalist camps, above all he feared legalism – which can be roughly defined as a commitment to rules untethered to principles.

The problem is that we can hide behind broad principles and thus avoid obeying the direct, rule-type commands of Christ and of other voices in Scripture. When we focus on principles, we are at risk of thinning out our moral instruction into vague generalities that do not require anything much from anybody. Thus, the preacher tells his people to love their neighbors but has nothing particular to say about loving that neighbor who is your husband when he is driving you crazy and you are considering divorce. What does love require of you in this particular situation or in all relevantly similar situations? Proclaimers of the gospel need to be particularly aware of the temptation to hide behind general principles in order to avoid giving offense to anyone who might be hearing us. The Scriptures are embarrassingly concrete and specific in their moral instruction. The Bible does indeed contain rules, and to say so does not make one a legalist. Meanwhile, to fail to say so can lead to considerable moral confusion. Thus, we turn briefly to rules.

The Second Floor: Rules

The great value of moral rules is their clarity and concreteness. "Feed the hungry" leaves little room for misunderstanding or evasion. The questions are reduced to two: Are we going to obey this command? If so, how exactly shall we implement that obedience?

Many preachers are uncomfortable with the concept of offering direct rule-type exhortation from the pulpit. We do not want to seem authoritarian, too rigid, or too dogmatic. Perhaps we hold the theological belief that the Christian faith is not "about" rules. There is the possibility that we are misunderstanding the Scripture at one point or another. We want to allow room for dialogue and difference of opinion. Just directly telling our congregants what the rules are may seem old-fashioned or out of step with the (post)modern temper. Perhaps it will inhibit our church's growth or its evangelistic outreach to seekers and other onlookers.

Yet the evidence is clear that in this time of moral conflict and confusion in our society, those Christian churches
that offer clear and concrete moral instruction are flourishing. A recent article in *Christianity Today* documented once
again the obvious numerical growth of evangelical churches
and contrasted that growth with the numerical decline of the
mainline.[18] One reason for the difference – a reason noted on
both sides of the evangelical/mainline divide – is the greater
clarity and specificity of moral teaching generally found on
the evangelical side of the fence. While some opponents de-
ride evangelicalism for its supposed lack of appreciation for
the moral "gray" areas of life, it seems clear that the people
in the pews hunger for as much clarity and direction from the
pulpit as we can responsibly offer. Churches that do not know
what they believe about morality, and do not exhibit anything
distinctively Christian in the way they live their lives, offer no
hope and no help to morally confused individuals in a morally
chaotic time.

This is not to say that fears related to the proclamation, and
especially the enforcement, of moral rules are completely un-
founded. Those fears are frequently based on an awareness of
the slide into a rigid and narrow legalism that has so frequently
characterized the more conservative churches, at least at an earlier period in American religious history. Postfundamentalists
have many horror stories to tell concerning this kind of legalism. The problems essentially cluster into three main areas: the
slide into a punitive authoritarianism, the narrowing of Christian morality into concern for only a very few areas of life (for
example, sex), and the continual piling on of nonscriptural and
increasingly absurd rules and regulations. Thus, one arrives at
the caricature – a historically well-rooted caricature – of the
red-faced preacher shouting at a handful of teenage girls in the
church one Sunday night for their sex-related sin of wearing
blue jeans or eye makeup. Many are the people who have been
lost to the church forever because of exposure to that sorry
approach to "the moral dimension of preaching."

When we speak of recovering the proclamation of biblical
moral rules, we mean something altogether different. It is certainly possible to avoid the errors that have plagued the church

in this area of its life. At the heart of a better approach, we think, is the use of something like the three-floor model we are talking about here. Any rules one would proclaim must be indisputably biblical: "Do not commit adultery"; "clothe the naked"; "do not gossip." They must be rules that are clearly grounded in broader biblical principles, as outlined above, such as neighbor love, justice, truthfulness, and the sacredness of human life. Indeed, perhaps the best way to avoid proclaiming a too narrow set of moral rules is to test your proclamation against the diverse and wide-ranging moral principles one finds in Scripture. Finally, these principle-grounded rules must themselves relate to a fully biblical and coherent view of the character and will of God. In preparation for any given sermon with rule-type content, ask the question, "Is the rule I am proclaiming today fully consistent with the character of God revealed by Jesus Christ?" In evaluating a year or a lifetime of sermons, ask the broader question – "Is the *sum total* of my proclamation of moral rules (and moral principles) painting an adequate picture of the character of God?"

One final word about rules is needed. Because the proclamation of moral rules is in fact so clear and concrete, the preacher should expect to encounter resistance from congregants every now and then. "God commands that we love our enemies, and we are not doing so, friends. This must change." "The Scripture requires that we feed the hungry." "God requires of us that we welcome persons of all races to our church, and there is resistance to this idea among us. This must stop." That kind of preaching will very likely stimulate anger. There are perhaps ways to soften its sharp edge. But, as one aspect of the moral dimension of preaching, it is not optional. It requires of the preacher the courage we discussed in chapter 1 – the willingness to pay the price of truthful biblical proclamation.

The Third Floor: Particular Judgments

There is yet one more level of moral proclamation. As we noted above, these are the particular moral judgments made from the pulpit concerning the issues facing a particular people of God in a particular time and place. Let us adapt our chart related to rules and principles and add this element to illuminate our meaning:

Principle	*Rule*	*Particular Judgment*
neighbor love	forgive one another	forgive the man who burned our church
justice	act on behalf of the stranger	protest the treatment plant in low-income area
sacredness of life	defend the innocent	write a letter to Congress about abortion bill
holiness	purify your thoughts of lust	do not visit new local strip joint
truthfulness	let your yes be yes	be honest about our racism problem
fidelity to covenant	do not commit adultery	establish these safeguards to prevent adultery

It is important to note a couple of vital characteristics of the particular judgment level as it applies to preaching. The first observation is the radical context – specificity of such judgments. A situation has emerged in your congregation or your community or your nation. As the preacher, you believe the Scripture speaks to that situation. You bring the particular situation into contact with the rule/principle/ground-of-meaning resources of Scripture, and after prayer and discernment, articulate a moral judgment and offer moral direction from the pulpit. The particular judgment level is essentially reserved – or at least functions best – for the local congregational preacher, whose daily ministry involves intimate contact with a particular people in time and space.

A second observation is that while both positive and negative biblical rules can lead to particular moral applications and judgments, the positively stated rules are those that tend to lead to the most fruitful and action-oriented particular judgments. If we teach the rule "Do not kill," then we are leading our people to be aware of what they should not do. There is no particular judgment that flows easily from that. But if we teach the rule, "defend the innocent," we are drawn toward specific action steps and particular judgments that will constitute obedience to that rule in this context. This is a good reminder to us to avoid sliding into a presentation of Christian morality that is solely negative and prohibitory in its orientation.

Finally, particular judgments must be viewed with appropriate caution and humility. They do not carry the same authority as the biblical rules or principles upon which we hope they are grounded. They are the preacher's best attempt to interpret the meaning of those rules and principles for his or her particular context. Quite sincere as he or she may be, the preacher may be wrong. John Stott is right in warning the preacher to focus primarily on opening up biblical principles for reflection and on shaping a Christian mind rather than on proposing, for example, precise and detailed political programs.[19] Likewise, even where particular judgments are appropriate, because of their profound specificity they are the moral teachings most likely to generate the fiercest opposition, as some of the examples given above should indicate. While humility is called for, so is courage in the face of inevitable opposition.

Moral Norms: For Whom? About What?

There is yet one final piece to the puzzle. We have offered a model for discussing the four kinds of moral norms that need attention if the moral dimension of preaching is to be addressed adequately. But we have not considered two closely related questions: *For whom* are these moral norms – theological framework, principles, rules, particular judgments – offered? Further, *about what* areas of the moral life are these norms addressed? We will consider both of these questions briefly, by way of concluding this attempt to reenvision the moral dimension of preaching.

As least three different answers to the first question are in regular circulation today and are reflected in Christian preaching about morality. Some offer moral instruction primarily to the Christian *individual*. Thus, moral rules and the principles that ground them are understood to be directed to the "person in the pew" who is struggling with the moral issues of life. In preparing sermons on morality, the preacher envisions the thoughtful or troubled layperson wrestling with the moral dilemmas of her or his life, and seeks to speak to that person.

Some of the examples given in the "particular judgment" section of the chart above clearly pertain to another possible audience – the gathered congregation as a whole. The preacher is not trying to help the individual determine what to do but instead is attending to the congregation: What should *we* do about relating to the man who burned our church building down, or about our congregational problem with racism, or about the sewage treatment plant that is about to be placed in a low-income section of town, or about the upcoming bill related to abortion?

Another audience is not to be found within the walls of the church at all. Sometimes the moral dimension of preaching addresses the society (or the world) and its leaders. When this is the case, the issue is not what *I* (the Christian) should do or what *we* (the congregation) should do, but what *they*, the nation's leaders, should do; or what *we*, the nation's citizens, should do. Again, this can sometimes reach a global level. To address environmental concerns, for example, we must sometimes discuss what they/global leaders/the world community should do.

Various ethicists have suggested that one or another of these audiences is the only appropriate recipient of ethical exhortation. There is a long tradition in Western moral philosophy of addressing moral instruction and reflection to the thoughtful individual. There is great value to this, for sometimes we do face critical moral decisions as individuals and need to be addressed as such. Yet, more recently, many ethicists have reminded us that Scripture most frequently addresses the *community* of faith, whether it be Israel (in the Old Testament), the disciples (in the Gospels), or a local church or churches (in the Epistles). There are indeed times when a preacher must address a congregation as a whole, not merely as disparate individuals who congregate therein. A strong case can be made that this audience should be the primary one. Yet there are also times when the moral dimension of preaching is best served by a look outward to the nation or to the world and its leaders. This is a particular genre of preaching – the public moral address – which the prophets pioneered and which cannot be allowed to disappear.

Thus, the wise preacher will run his or her preaching through this particular grid as well as the others, asking, "Is my proclamation directed to the right audiences in the right proportion?" If the audience is always the individual Christian, the congregational moral sense, as well as a broader social ethical vision, will be underdeveloped. If the audience is always the congregation, struggling individuals will find little nourishment, and again the world beyond the congregation may disappear from moral view. Finally, if the audience too frequently is America as a whole, the preacher may fall prey to creating an overdeveloped national moral sensitivity and an underdeveloped moral ethos closer to home, in the congregation and in the individuals and families that constitute it. This last focal audience is also the one most likely to generate the kind of angry and politicized finger pointing into which the moral dimension of preaching sometimes degenerates.

The second question was "About what?" What arenas of life should the moral dimension of preaching address?

Some ethicists, and preachers influenced by this particular line of thought emphasize *hard decisions about moral norms and beliefs.* The moral dimension of life, and thus of preaching, is that arena of existence in which I or we must make "hard choices" about what to believe and teach, given competing moral viewpoints. A large number of ethics texts approach their task in this way. Preaching of this type might ask such questions as: "What should I or we *believe* and *teach* about euthanasia? About cloning? About abortion in case of rape?" A pro-con analysis might be offered of biblical evidence on either "side" of these tough questions. The goal is to arrive at a biblical/Christian *perspective* and then to teach that faithfully. It is possible to focus "hard decision" ethics at the individual, church, national, or even international level, as discussed above: "What should I/we/they believe and teach about race?" But regardless of the answer to the "for whom" question, the "about what" answer is clear: Ethical direction is about what to teach and believe concerning hard moral quandaries.

An entirely different approach argues that ethics is about *character*, not decisions. Character has to do with moral being, with that core of moral agency and identity from which, it can be argued, all decisions and actions actually flow. To ask about character is to explore what kind of person I am supposed to be, what kind of people *we* are supposed to be – as Christian communities or even as a nation state – and even what kind of people *they* (government leaders, business executives, and so on) are supposed to be. Here the focus shifts profoundly from the solving of moral quandaries to the nurture of moral persons and communities who will bring well-formed character into the wide range of moral quandaries that we face today. Such character is constituted by a range of moral virtues, such as love, joy, peace, patience, and other attributes that Paul describes as "fruit of the Spirit" (Galatians 5:22-23). Preaching focused on character asks which attributes are normative for the Christian or Christian community and explores ways to nurture persons characterized by such virtues.

Finally, it is possible to answer the "about what" question in terms of moral *practices*. If moral practices are the subject of ethics, the focus shifts from what convictions to teach/believe and what virtues to nurture to what *behaviors* to *perform*. An emphasis on practices drives the church back to a focus on the concrete behaviors that it daily performs or fails to perform: feeding the hungry, clothing the naked, publicly siding with the oppressed, making peace with enemies, forgiving one another, sharing the Eucharist, baptizing new believers, and so on. A recovery of the moral dimension of preaching, in this view, will involve clear explanation and ultimately demonstration of what Michael Cartwright has called "apostolic practices of discipleship."[20] Advocates of this approach insist that Jesus, among other biblical figures, did not so much teach moral convictions or moral values as he taught and demonstrated a set of moral practices, which the faithful church will likewise take upon itself.

The moral dimension of preaching is best served by the effort to find a place for all three kinds of answers to the "about what" question. There are occasions in which individuals, congregations, and societies do face hard moral choices, and preaching needs to address such occasions with clear direction. The people of God do need to know what we must *believe* about such issues as abortion, the environment, and euthanasia.

Coming to the right convictions about such matters is not the end of the story, but it is an important part of it.

Such convictions need to be demonstrated in the form of "apostolic practices," as well as what we might call "postapostolic-yet-faithful practices." The moral dimension of preaching is incomplete without attention to these practices, for the Christian faith is a way of life, not just a set of beliefs. Mere doctrinalism, whether in theology or in ethics, unaccompanied by the performance of the acts of discipleship, quickly strangles the vitality of a people of God. It seems to us that the lack of such practices as feeding the poor, standing with the oppressed, forgiving the one who offends, remaining faithfully married, living in a sexually chaste manner, and so on, is perhaps the gravest moral failure of the contemporary North American church. The clear witness of the Scripture is that the early church thrived and attracted its thousands of new converts in large part due to the revolutionary quality of its way of life under the Spirit of God, not just because of its theological and moral beliefs.

Finally, the current emphasis on character rightly reminds us that we do what we are — "out of the overflow of [one's] heart" come actions both good and evil (Luke 6:45). The classic doctrine of sanctification reminds us that God is at work transforming the heart, will, and mind — that is, the character — of the believing Christian. Preachers all too infrequently attend in any kind of systematic way to Christian character, which is the fount of the kinds of moral decisions and practices that bring glory to God.

Conclusion

We have covered a considerable amount of ground in this chapter. We hope that along the way we have aided the reader in reenvisioning the moral dimension of preaching in its various aspects. We hope you will use this grid to evaluate your current approach to preaching as well as to serve as a guide to the planning of preaching in the days ahead.

NOTES

1. The overall moral grid we are developing in this chapter draws heavily on David P. Gushee and Glen H. Stassen, *Christian Ethics as Following Jesus,* forthcoming from InterVarsity Press.

2. The distinction between "abiding and universal laws," on the one hand, and "temporary, specific commands," on the other, is made by – among others – Christian ethicist Lewis B. Smedes. See Smedes, *Mere Morality* (Grand Rapids: Eerdmans, 1983), 246, n. 3.

3. Some homileticians are so impressed by the significance of the prophets for preaching that they essentially identify the prophetic material with the moral dimension of Scripture. See Jesse Jai McNeil, *The Preacher-Prophet in Mass Society,* rev. ed. (Nashville: Townsend, 1993). Among the good recent studies of the use of the prophets in preaching one finds James Ward and Christine Ward, *Preaching from the Prophets* (Nashville: Abingdon, 1995).

4. Kelly Miller Smith, *Social Crisis Preaching* (Atlanta: Mercer, 1984), 14.

5. Smedes, *Mere Morality,* 245, n. 2.

6. One germane work that reflects this strong emphasis on narrative is Ronald J. Sider and Michael A. King, *Preaching about Life in a Threatening World* (Philadelphia: Westminster, 1987), especially chapter 3.

7. Thomas G. Long, *The Witness of Preaching* (Louisville, Ky.: Westminster/John Knox, 1989), 40.

8. Arthur Van Seters, ed., *Preaching as a Social Act: Theology and Practice* (Nashville: Abingdon, 1988), 252.

9. Ibid., 249.

10. Bryan Chapell offers an encouraging move in the direction of a focus on Christ with his *Christ-Centered Preaching* (Grand Rapids: Baker, 1994). However, we do not find in that work adequate attention to the actual life and teachings of Christ.

11. Thomas G. Long and Edward Farley, eds., *Preaching as a Theological Task* (Louisville, Ky.: Westminster, 1996).

12. For just such an approach to the doctrine of Creation, see Donald Coggan, *Preaching: The Sacrament of the Word* (New York: Crossroad, 1988), chap. 7. For examples of approaches emphasizing the key theological themes of Scripture, broadly understood, see Jesse Jai McNeil, *The Preacher-Prophet in Mass Society,* especially 83-84, and Samuel D. Proctor, *Preaching about Crises in the Community* (Philadelphia: Westminster, 1988).

13. Thomas H. Troeger, "The Social Power of Myth as a Key to Preaching on Social Issues," in Van Seters, ed., *Preaching as a Social Act,* 205-6.

14. James H. Harris, *Preaching Liberation* (Minneapolis: Fortress, 1995), ix.

15. Smith, *Social Crisis Preaching,* cf. 12–15.

16. See Justo L. Gonzalez and Catherine Gunsalus Gonzalez, *Liberation Preaching* (Nashville: Abingdon, 1980).

17. McNeil, *Preacher-Prophet in Mass Society,* 81.

18. Tony Campolo, moderator, "The Spirit Hasn't Left the Mainline," *Christianity Today* 41, no. 9 (August 11, 1997), 14–20.

19. John R. W. Stott, *Between Two Worlds* (Grand Rapids: Eerdmans, 1982), 167.

20. Michael G. Cartwright, "Radical Reform, Radical Catholicity: John Howard Yoder's Vision of the Faithful Church," in John Howard Yoder, *The Royal Priesthood* (Grand Rapids: Eerdmans, 1994), 1.

CHAPTER THREE

A New Approach to the Task

Ethical Preachers and Ethical Preaching

Having considered the ethical content of today's sermons with a view toward reenvisioning preaching on the moral life, we can now turn our attention to crafting a practical model for such preaching. This kind of model arises from one's definition of preaching. We are not suggesting that every preacher has settled on a formal definition of preaching. Rather, we are convinced that every preacher acts, at the very least, out of a personal, informal definition of the preaching event. Such a definition may be so deeply ingrained in a preacher's life that he or she is not consciously aware of it. Yet that very definition gives shape to the preacher's task. By giving shape to the task at hand, it also establishes the limits of the preacher's thinking about his or her craft. In this chapter, then, we will consider a definition of preaching, look at the inescapably personal dimension of preaching as it relates to the moral life, and offer a practical model for ethical — that is, ethically sensitive — preaching.

Toward a Definition of Preaching

In his work *Between Two Worlds: The Art of Preaching in the Twentieth Century,* John Stott reaches into his bag of rich metaphors in search of a definition of preaching. Stott's concern is for the preacher, one with an almost impossible task. For, according to Stott, the preacher is seeking ways to communicate truth across a vast cultural gulf. Preaching is the art of bridge building. "Our task is to enable God's revealed truth to flow out of the Scriptures into the lives of the men and women of today."[1] Renowned nineteenth-century preacher Phillips Brooks defined preaching as the conveying of "truth through personality."[2] Brooks' definition, though not fully adequate in itself, has been the basis of many later attempts to come to an understanding of this most complex and unique activity.

Modern society's emphasis on the visual and deemphasis on the spoken or written word calls for a reexamination of our definitions. It may well be time for modification. Indeed, Stott took seriously the role of society in shaping the preacher's work as was suggested by his definition of the preaching task. The preacher must be aware of two primary responsibilities. The first is to work with the revealed truth of God. No preacher is competent who neglects the serious task of handling the biblical text. The preacher must also bring that text into the contemporary setting. The congregation gathers to worship God, to discover God's will for their lives, to gain the resources needed for their spiritual journey. The key word is *gathers*. When our congregants gather together, they carry with them their combined hurts, fears, failures, and frustrations as well as their hopes, successes, strengths, joys, and dreams. But we Christians often mask our condition – seeking to hide from each other and maybe even from God – when we enter the church building on an average Sunday. Yet our condition does not change, nor our need for resources for the journey.

Thus, a very useful thumbnail definition of the preaching task is *to contextualize the truth of God*. This is the work of the preacher. It implies two possible ways in which preaching can miss the mark. First, if the preacher fails to bring the truth of God over the "bridge" of two millennia and into the contemporary setting, the congregation is left, at best, with a well-prepared Bible study or history lesson. They may or may not have the means within themselves to apply that biblical truth to their daily lives; and if they do, they certainly have not received those means from the preacher. On the other hand, when the preacher spends all available time in the current context, without sufficient attention to the biblical text, the congregation receives some pleasant, interesting, or relevant thoughts but no word from God.

To define preaching as contextualizing the truth of God focuses the preaching task on an ethical plane. The Scripture, as we have tried to show, is full of moral content; meanwhile, the world in which we live presents us almost daily with moral issues demanding our attention. Thus, whether we move from our context to the Scripture, or from Scripture to our context — both are acceptable — the moral dimension of our task is apparent.[3] Preaching void of ethical content fails the most basic of tests. It has not contextualized God's Word for a waiting people.

Ethics and the Integrity of the Preacher

Many have observed the inescapably personal dimension of preaching. Preaching that is unrelated to a minister's own personhood is inauthentic, even farcical. This is perhaps most clearly the case with regard to the moral dimension of preaching. The minister is called upon to live out those moral convictions he or she proclaims and to proclaim only those moral convictions that genuinely reflect his or her own beliefs. There is no way around it. If we do not live out the moral convictions we proclaim, we are the worst of hypocrites. On the other hand, if we proclaim as moral truths things that we do not genuinely believe, we are liars. To add another layer of complexity, if we proclaim and even live out moral convictions that are unexamined or unbiblical, we court disaster. We have known preachers who are sincerely racist in word and deed. There is no hypocrisy here — just morally repugnant consistency.

The preacher, as ethical spokesperson, is both a proclaimer of moral convictions to a congregation gathering on a regular basis for worship and at the same time a product of moral convictions gleaned from encounters across a lifetime. One can picture ethics as a powerful, surging reservoir in the preacher's life. That reservoir is constantly reshaping the contours of the preacher's personal thought on ethical issues. Out of that reservoir the preacher draws regularly to share insight with the congregation.

The Call Experience

God creates preachers out of the raw material of humanity. Of particular importance is what we have come to understand as the "call" experience. That experience varies with each individual, but one truth remains constant: The call experience is basic in the making of a preacher.

I (Bob Long) have several pieces of cross-stitching in my office. Some are gifts from members of congregations I served in earlier years, and others are pieces produced by my wife. The beautiful finished product is possible because of the strong, regular material underneath the individual stitches. In a similar way, the call experience of the preacher is the strong fiber holding together all other characteristics of that ministry and life. Each calling is unique, just as is each individual. Some individuals can describe their call experience in great detail. Others have difficulty putting it into words. Some report the assistance of a trusted spiritual adviser and friend in discovering their calling. Others discover their calling alone with God. Regardless of the particulars of the call from God, that call is the underlying factor in forming and sustaining the preacher. Without it, the demands of ministry will force a would-be minister into other work.

While the call is divine as well as unique, it is ever a call to preparation. God calls individuals from a broad cross section of life. Some are from humble means. For them, there may be little chance for formal education. Others have the benefit of the finest seminary training. Still the minister is always in the preparation mode, seeking out opportunities to become better informed, better trained, and better equipped because of a desire to communicate effectively with the congregation. Every preacher is endowed with a set of personal gifts and traits. These traits can be enhanced and broadened but only at the cost of disciplining oneself. Halford Luccock, in his book *In the Minister's Workshop*, picturesquely entitled one chapter "To

Toil Like a Miner Under a Landslide." That is our obligation. For
Luccock, the preacher's preparation is a tremendously difficult
task.[4] Preparation is made especially difficult because members
of the congregation often expect the minister to be available
for any need they feel. The demands on the preacher's time can
be enormous. Holding to a disciplined schedule of study can
strain the preacher's relationships with some in the congregation. However, the cost of yielding to every demand for time
will mean that too often the preacher will be ill-prepared to
preach on Sunday. The minister must protect the quality of that
worship hour, because that time allows the minister to touch
the greatest number of lives.

God's claim on the preacher is a call to a lifetime of service.
Leadership in ministry means serving, as Jesus instructed his
disciples (Mark 10:35–45). American culture offers a variety of
models for leadership. Few, however, are examples of leading
through service. Yet that model is the very one employed by the
Lord Jesus. "Whoever wants to become great among you must
be your servant, and whoever wants to be first must be slave of
all. For even the Son of Man did not come to be served, but to
serve, and to give his life as a ransom for many" (Mark 10:43–
45). Preachers lose the moral platform from which to lead a
congregation whenever they refuse to do tasks that are somehow beneath them. This does not mean that ministers must do
everything themselves, but it does suggest that they are the primary models for service in the church. Our preaching of the
moral dimension of Scripture will have integrity and authority
when our life reflects Christ's vision of servanthood.

God's call is also an invitation, indeed a command, to
become a lifelong student of the Bible. Before one can contextualize God's truth to a hungry congregation, one must
understand the text of Scripture. How the preacher approaches
personal Bible study is in itself a moral issue. There are preachers whose understanding of ethical issues is clearly much more
a product of social mores than of scriptural truth. All of us
who stand in pulpits need to develop a "filter" through which
we can read the Bible while extracting our cultural bias. Without such a filter our reading of the Bible becomes a slave to
our social setting, leading to such moral calamities as the white

Christian affirmation of apartheid in South Africa and of slavery and segregation in the United States. How easily we slip into this trap! There is no automatic alarm that sounds when we are substituting culture and prejudice for the Word of God.

How does the preacher construct such a filter? We suggest that the proper starting point is in construction and use of the moral grid outlined in chapter 2. The preacher can employ the grid in his or her reading of biblical texts in much the same way that other basic questions of the text are asked. Preachers are taught to come before the biblical text asking such questions as: For whom was this text originally intended? What type of literature is this? Are there any noteworthy historical references? Adding the moral grid to this approach to the text is not an encumbrance. It merely involves adding such questions as: What does this passage reveal about the character and will of God? What moral principles are at stake in this text? Are there particular rules or practices for the Christian life that are mandated here? What particular moral judgments related to my context are suggested by this text? Such questions, asked in the study process on a regular basis, can only enrich the moral dimension of preaching.

The Humanity of the Preacher

What preacher does not abhor the caricaturing of ministry we see so often in society? In truth, though, we are often our own worst enemies in this regard. Whenever we fail to be honest about our own humanity, for whatever reason, we bolster the case of the caricaturists. Preachers are humans first. Once we heard of a pastor who cut his lawn each week in his Sunday suit in order not to appear in public in anything other than his normal "uniform." It is amazing to us whenever we encounter preachers who have seemingly lost a sense of their own humanity. They have become so absorbed in the role of the preacher that the human being who once filled that role and was distinguishable from that role no longer can be found.

The humanity of the preacher includes what are sometimes unpleasant incidents from one's past. We cannot undo our past, but we can own it. Where our past is embarrassing, we must confess our sins, accept responsibility, and work to remedy past wrongs. All of us have attributes of character that, when channeled properly, will shape our preaching constructively. Peter was impetuous. While it sometimes caused him to act without thinking, it also led him to moments of brilliant insight, such as the occasion at the coast of Caesarea recorded in Matthew 16:13–20. The apostle Paul showed strength of character, not only in his preaching, but in his dealings with those who opposed him. Yet he was not without his faults – a truth that ought to embolden us. God can make use even – perhaps especially – of our weaknesses for his purposes (2 Corinthians 12:9).

A preacher's human side cannot be neglected without grave consequence. Caring for one's physical health was recognized as long ago as the classic preaching text by John A. Broadus: "The long hours in the study should be balanced by a careful diet and regular exercise."[5] V. L. Stanfield suggested that a preacher's exercise regimen could easily be combined with pastoral duties.[6] Preachers who have no outside interests become dull to the congregation. Hobbies invigorate ministers, make them more well rounded, and give them connections to the community. In the movie *Teacher's Pet*, Clark Gable played a hard-bitten newspaper editor. In one scene, he teaches a young aspiring reporter the value of education as a means to becoming a more well-rounded individual. "You'll find out there are a lot of other places in the world besides this city room. You only spend eight hours a day here. If you're lucky, you spend eight hours sleeping, eight hours working. That leaves eight hours more to talk to other people about other things. If all you know is newspapers, you'll always be excusing yourself and leaving the table."[7] That is good advice for preachers, because we often find ourselves in settings other than the church and with people other than church people, who are watching how we conduct ourselves in those other arenas. If the only place we are comfortable is in the pulpit, we will diminish the impact of our ministry.

A preacher is also a family member. It is most unfortunate when preachers' families are neglected, as so often happens. Taking care of one's family requires an unshakable time commitment. It is truly sad to see ministers' children who have no desire to follow God's will for their lives because of their experience of neglect while growing to adulthood. As a minister, your spouse deserves the best portion of your life. The vows you and your spouse exchanged at the altar were not nullified by a call from a congregation – although both you and your congregation are tempted to forget this sometimes.

The minister is also a member of society. We suggest that you reserve some energy for service to the community beyond the walls of the local church. While some members of the church may complain, the majority will be glad to see their minister involved in the community. That involvement can take many forms. Some volunteer to help in schools. Others fill roles in community human needs areas. Some preachers' love for the arts has led them to involvement in community choruses or theaters. Every community has various agencies in which ministers can find fulfillment from public service either from serving on the organization's governing board or from hands-on service. Such opportunities make the pastor a richer, more complete individual. Often the dividends are noticed in the pulpit.

The final component of the preacher's character we will consider is personal moral convictions. As we have hinted above, the minister must continually scrutinize his or her moral convictions and values. Failing to do so often leads the preacher to proclaim as biblical truths values that are actually developed from other sources, such as economic self-interest.

While many issues could be explored in this regard, we want to focus here on the issue of world-view and its connection to moral convictions. A world-view can be roughly defined as one's understanding of the world, one's place in the world, and how both relate to God. A world-view is a vision of life. The concept is really nothing new to those of us in ministry. Preachers have worked out of a point of view about the world from New Testament times until today. Our goal should be that our world-view would conform to the biblical world-view; that we would enter the biblical story and make it our own. However, this is all too infrequently the case. What usually happens – to preachers as well as to Christian laypeople – is that our world-view is far more cultural than biblical.

A good example of this comes from Christianity in the American South. Regrettably, in the South the (white) preacher's viewpoint was so wedded to southern culture as to be practically the same. The preacher became a faithful mouthpiece of cultural values. There was no reason to examine or question "the southern way." However, the explosion of change taking place in American culture in the South has shattered the monolithic culture that once existed there. Only now have we (here we speak as Southern Baptists) begun to see how captive to culture we really were and how disastrous were the consequences of that captivity.

Today's preachers work in a context that calls for a strange, sometimes uneasy connection to the world at large. Ministers are members of society; they pay taxes, educate their children, and consume products and services like every other member of society. On the other hand, preachers stand as spokespersons for the kingdom of God in a society frequently characterized by anti-kingdom values and practices. Of all Christians, preachers are the ones who must be able to discern most clearly the gap between culture and Scripture. In order to do so, a healthy, critical distance must be kept from the temptation to embrace the world, its goods, and its values. Because truth is lived at least as much as it is taught, a preacher's character, integrity, and authenticity Monday through Saturday are perhaps more significant than any words that might be spoken from the pulpit on Sunday.

Ethics and the Craft of the Preacher

Having examined the humanity and character of the preacher, we now turn to a practical consideration of the ways the preacher practices his or her craft. The first thing to be said is that our character and our craft are intertwined and perhaps ultimately indistinguishable. Our preaching emerges from our personhood, as we have indicated. But still, there are tools of the trade, elements of our craft, that need separate consideration.

Again we search for a useful analogy. Perhaps it will be helpful to consider the preacher plying his craft in somewhat the same way a master chef prepares a dish. The chef works systematically from the pantry to the place setting. The finished product is a combination of science and art. In the same way, sermon development has been described as both science and art. We shall consider the pantry of our "kitchen" to be the ethical/theological materials from which the preacher draws the raw ingredients for the sermon. But no master chef simply puts the raw ingredients on a plate to be served to guests. Neither should the preacher be content to simply pour out the raw stuff of a potential sermon before a gathered congregation. A number of steps transform the raw materials into a finished product. In much the same way, the preacher takes the raw materials and works them into a final sermon form. Interestingly, one often finds the same basic ingredients in totally different dishes. One might label this part of the process for the preacher as "Soup or Souffle – From Idea to Formal Sermon Form." If the master chef is so inclined, he becomes responsible for fixing not just one dish but rather a balanced, healthy approach to eating. Likewise, the minister in a parish setting is truly responsible for a balanced, healthy approach to meeting the spiritual needs of the congregation. In that way, the minister's preaching schedule is like plotting a well-balanced diet.

The Preacher's Tools

The Bible is at the heart of the preacher's "pantry." The preacher builds an ethical/theological framework initially from Bible study. "The higher our view of the Bible, the more painstaking and conscientious our study of it should be."[8] Everyone who stands in a pulpit to preach from the Bible, regardless of his or her level of training, faces the issue of exegesis. In their book *Building Sermons to Meet People's Needs*, Harold Bryson and James C. Taylor define exegesis as the "study of words, phrases, and the grammatical relationships in a passage."[9] This simple definition will serve us for the moment. What does the preacher need in order to produce a proper exegesis? The tools of the craft center around the Bible and our ability to better understand the text.

The well-stocked "pantry" of the preacher will have the types of commentaries, linguistic tools, and biblical translations the individual is competent to manage. Ethically based sermons are first and foremost biblical. The starting point for a sermon dealing with a moral issue is the same as for any other sermon – a clear understanding of the text.

The preacher should use some thought and care in developing his or her library. At the center of that library will be a rich variety of Bible translations. Our bias will show for a moment. We believe every American preacher would be well served with at least three different English translations of the Bible. If limited to three, we would choose the King James Version, the Revised Standard Version (or the New Revised Standard Version), and the New International Version. Preaching is an oral activity. Years ago I (Bob Long) benefited from a wonderful professor of oral interpretation in college. I still remember her claim that anyone who could master the public reading of the King James Version of the Bible was competent to stand and read in a public setting. The discipline of practicing to read with appropriate feeling from the King James Version aids the preacher in preparation. Remember that the first impression you give of your mastery of your subject is as you read the text for that particular sermon. I would also choose the Revised Standard Version of the Bible for its trustworthy interpretation of the Old Testament. While it is true that there are other versions with a smoother translation into today's vernacular, the shades of nuance found by reading from the Revised Standard Version have proven very helpful in sermon preparation. Going into the pulpit, the preacher should have a version of Scripture that the greatest percentage of the congregation can hear and understand. The preacher should remember that not all present will have an open text before them. What many will grasp of the text is what they hear as it is read.

Today's preacher has a plethora of linguistic tools to aid in sermon development. Again it is most important to match the tool to the skill level of the individual minister. While it might be ideal to suggest a basic level of training in the biblical languages as a prerequisite for the preacher, it is currently impractical to do so. Still, every preacher can enrich the sermon by building some type of linguistic tools into his or her library. These will range from simple one-volume word studies to complete Greek and Hebrew texts with appropriate dictionaries and lexicons. One rule never to be violated is for each of us to remain within our own skill level.

The preacher's library will certainly grow in the number of commentaries used over the course of time. Care should be the watchword here or else too many of the minister's financial resources will be absorbed in volumes that are of little benefit. There is no "best" system for obtaining these volumes. Some preachers enjoy the advantage of living near theological libraries, but many live beyond the practical range of such resources. For them, the option will be to purchase the commentaries needed. One systematic approach is to determine a particular book of the Bible on which to focus attention. Spend some time browsing the available volumes written on that book. Then purchase a minimum of three. One should be a solid, general work on the subject. The second should be a book written by an author whose background is different from yours. This gives you a chance to see an approach to the text distinct from yours. For instance, a Baptist preacher might purchase a commentary written by someone from the Reformed tradition or from a Roman Catholic background. No book will capture all the truth of the text. One need not fear a different understanding of a text based on a different faith tradition just as one is not compelled to accept such an interpretation simply by reading it. The third commentary might be a very technical text, one that deals with aspects of textual criticism and details of the biblical language. This type of commentary is recommended particularly for those inevitable, obscure texts that crop up in every book of the Bible. Exegesis begins as the preacher comes to understand the text in its setting. Still the preacher's preparation is not complete at this point.

The preacher's library needs salting with a comprehensive, systematic theology, of which there are a multitude available. The same advice we articulated above applies here – seek out a range of theological voices for breadth and depth. In this case, though, we do recommend that you develop particularly a collection of resources that reflect your own central theological stance. Additionally, a portion of the preacher's reading and studying time should be devoted to general reading materials. These include but are not limited to daily newspapers, journals from any field of study of interest to the minister, contemporary magazines, and contemporary and classic books, both fiction and nonfiction. The preacher will stand before congregations whose collective interests will stretch the ability of any speaker to understand. The better read the minister becomes, the greater the probability of making a strong connection with the individuals in the pews and of being prepared to address their most important moral concerns.

To preach adequately on such moral issues requires a broader range of resources than one commonly finds in a preacher's library. The basic building blocks for ethics-oriented preaching include two types of materials: exegetical works focusing on moral issues (war, sex, marriage, and the like) or themes (love, justice, peace, holiness) addressed in Scripture, and ethical studies of contemporary issues (abortion, racism, euthanasia, gambling, and so on). Dozens of excellent recent works can be found of both types, and some combine the genres. Generally speaking, the scholarly division of labor leaves the former work to biblical scholars with ethical interests and the latter to self-identified Christian ethicists. The biblical/exegetical studies are best suited to helping the preacher move from text to contemporary situation, while the contemporary ethical works are most helpful for moving in the other direction.

Three other types of materials bear mentioning as well. First, just as there are numerous dictionaries, concordances, and other reference tools for biblical exegesis, today there are similar tools available in Christian ethics, such as *The Westminster Dictionary of Christian Ethics*. [10] We strongly recommend that every preacher acquire one or two such dictionaries. Hopefully, the problem of keeping such reference tools from rapid obsolescence will soon be solved by the move to updatable CD-ROMs.

Another type of resource for the ethically responsible

preacher is the plethora of excellent nontheological works on contemporary moral issues. Many times – perhaps even most of the time – the best current analyses of such problems as race, poverty, divorce, and the environment will not be found in the religion section of the bookstore or library, but instead in such places as the social science, government, African-American, family life, and current affairs departments. One could wish, as we certainly do, for a better collection of Christian treatments of such subjects. But with proper theological/moral sifting, these other kinds of works are a powerful and positive addition to one's ethical "pantry." One helpful hint: Invest about forty dollars a year to purchase the annual federal government *Statistical Abstract of the United States*, now in its 117th edition.[11] This treasure trove, now available in either traditional text or CD-ROM form, is an invaluable source of accurate information concerning the state of the society in which we live. If you want *reliable* data concerning the abortion rate, drug use, the shape of the American family, or nearly anything else of moral interest that can be quantified, this is the place to look.

Finally, in the era of the information superhighway, one cannot fail to mention the Internet as a resource for the ethical dimension of preaching. On nearly any issue one could care to address from the pulpit, there exist one or more significant websites. Some of these are related to universities and seminaries, some to advocacy and interest groups, some to interested individuals, and some to government agencies. Of course, the Internet presents the great challenge of separating the wheat from the chaff. One could easily be looking for reliable data on a sermon about the Holocaust, for example, and unwittingly end up at a website run by Holocaust deniers. Our advice is to consult a cyber-wise reference librarian and test whatever you find on the Internet against reliable outside sources.

Of course, the general reading discussed earlier – magazines, books, newspapers, and so on – should be read with a particular eye to ethical concerns. Not a day goes by in which the daily newspaper does not fail to contain rich (if frequently depressing) material for ethical reflection. Few things are as incomprehensible as a preacher who does not read and reflect upon the newspaper. Ideally, of course, the minister will read more deeply in current affairs than the pages of the local news-paper, but the paper is an indispensable part of the overall information flow.

A popular contemporary addition to the preacher's prepara-tion is the development of a small group of ministerial peers with whom the minister can have regular dialogue. (Sometimes such groups consist of laypeople and can be found within the congregation.) These groups frequently meet for the sole pur-pose of sermon discussion and enhancement. The advantages are obvious. The preacher is able to think in theological terms with others whose vocation is similar. This is rare in today's so-ciety and is a help to anyone within such a group. They are able to consider aspects of the text, contemporary news, trends in the life and work of the church, and so on, all with a view to-ward sermon preparation. They may even borrow phrases and exchange illustrations.

Nevertheless, there are some inherent difficulties caused by dependence on a peer group. Because, as Brooks noted, preach-ing is the conveying of truth through personality, the pulpit personality must ultimately be our own. When the congrega-tion gathers to hear a message, they have a right to believe that the words will be the work of the preacher rather than a cobbling together of the thoughts of a committee or the borrowing of sermons from a textbook. Nowhere will these inherent problems be more glaring than with ethical issues. A group of like-minded ministerial peers likely will form a con-sensus. As preachers, the transparent nature of our work will and should display our own struggle with the ethical issues. If our preaching is the result of a group effort, its ethical content may be muddled or watered down.

Still, a library alone, however well developed, does not ex-haust the preacher's "pantry." The most important component necessary to building an ethical repertoire for preaching is the preacher's *mind*. Part of the ministerial caricature that is so devastating to our work is the all too frequently accurate image of the intellectually lazy preacher who hasn't had a new idea in decades. We cannot rely on musty old seminary notes and rickety old theological truisms if we have any hope of contex-tualizing the truth of God. Instead, we must keep our minds active, refreshed, and engaged, both in asking fresh questions of the biblical text and in encountering our world in all of its daily pain and glory.

From Idea to Final Sermon Form

Let us turn now to consider the practical matter of mixing the raw ingredients of an ethical sermon into a coherent and even artful message. Each minister develops, over time, a preferred style of sermon. Traditionally sermon styles are classified as expository, textual, or topical. Topical sermons receive their start from a topic picked by the preacher. The sermon may or may not be grounded in any scriptural text. Instead, the major divisions within the sermon are developed by the subject, that is, the topic of the sermon, not the text. Topical sermons generally are out of favor among evangelicals today, yet they are sometimes the only way to fully address a contemporary moral issue, such as cloning, that is not addressed directly in the Bible.

Textual sermons differ greatly from topical sermons. Textual sermons are rooted in a text of Scripture. V. L. Stanfield suggested that the commonly accepted way of classifying sermons is by structure. According to his definition, a textual sermon is one whose major divisions are lifted from the biblical text.[12] In the textual sermon those divisions are generally implied, not specified.

The sermon style mostly preferred among evangelicals today is the expository sermon, although as recently as 1979 when Stanfield revised John Broadus's classic work on preaching, he reported the expository sermon to be the most neglected type of sermon.[13] In the 1940s, reflecting on the state of preaching over the first half of the century, James Stewart pled for a return to expository preaching. He called it "the greatest need of the hour."[14] Stanfield defined expository sermons as those whose major divisions as well as the exploration of those divisions are lifted from the text.[15] In the expository sermon, those divisions are generally lifted out of the text along with the major subpoints within each division.

While Stanfield defined sermon types based on structure, others have classified sermon types in different ways. Paul

Scherer, in *For We Have This Treasure*, identified four types of sermons: doctrinal, expository, ethical, and evangelical. Then he confused the issue by saying, "Let me only say again that I have never preached or heard read a sermon worthy of the name which was not to a greater or less degree all of these together."[16] Such confusion led Harold Bryson to formulate what he calls the eclectic definition of expository preaching. "Expository preaching involves the art of preaching a series of sermons either consecutively or selectively from a Bible book. Each sermon within the series needs to expose a biblical truth, and each sermon may also have different homiletical forms and any amount of Scripture for a text."[17]

Bryson is correct. Expository preaching should be seen as more than a style determined by structure. Indeed, the structure a sermon takes is one of the least important considerations for the preacher. The sermon, whether in series or standing alone, should expose before the congregation a biblical reality. That is why we suggest one final sermon style, the thematic sermon. Thematic sermons blend textual and expository elements together. As is the case with Bryson's definition, form is secondary. Content matters first. Next, the preacher should concern himself with shaping that content in a winsome way.

Thematic sermons are wonderful vehicles for delivering ethically based truth. The theme, not only of the sermon but of the entire worship service, can be structured around the ethical truth. Indeed, thematic sermons allow the whole worship service to flow from beginning to end toward the one theme. American culture is geared to process information gathered around one dominant point or theme. The congregation that experiences a well-crafted thematic worship service will be drawn into the theme easily. It is not unlike the evening television fare people are accustomed to absorbing. Yes, absorb is the proper word. Television engages the viewer at such a basic level that messages are easily encoded without drawing attention to the process. The viewer watches a selection while messages bombard the subconsciousness. The results can be quite dramatic. The same process can become the preacher's tool. Working in concert with the minister of music or other worship leaders, the preacher can construct a worship event around the theme selected for a given sermon. The public prayers, music (instrumental as well as vocal, congregational, and special), testimonies, and dramatic interpretations can point toward where the sermon will conclude.

With the stage set, we turn our attention to the sermon itself. While he or she is in the study, the preacher should be able to offer, in one sentence, the essence of the biblical text under consideration. Of course, more will be said in the pulpit about the text. However, the preacher must understand its central truth so well that it can be distilled into one simple sentence. Why such effort? Many scriptural passages have multiple strands of thought. If we cannot distill the text into one sentence, eliminating the strands of thought which, though true, do not pertain to the direction we intend to go, the result will be an unfocused sermon. With one thought clearly in mind, the sermon can expand without straying off our intended course. Understanding the text on such a basic level will afford the preacher with a touchstone in preparation. By regularly coming back to that one sentence, the preacher can keep a sharp focus on the central theme for the sermon.

The second step in the process is what Bryson and Taylor call the proposition or "essence of the sermon in a sentence" (ESS).[18] Synthesizing the text into one sentence is one thing. Being able to boil the essence of the *sermon* down to a single sentence is quite another. The difference between these two tasks is akin to the difference between understanding a premise and applying it. Some questions for the preacher in the study may prove helpful: What do I want to do with this particular sermon? What are the dominant truths from this passage as they apply to contemporary life? Do the members of my congregation struggle with this particular biblical truth? If so, how? What kind of application does this text allow? Regarding this biblical truth, what is the greatest need of the congregation? Clarifying how you will use the text in a single sentence opens many of the possible avenues for the sermon. This is probably the most effective way the preacher has of ensuring a single pursuit of one of those avenues. Following these two steps – distilling the text into one sentence and then stating the essence of the sermon in one sentence – will allow us to sharpen the focus of any sermon as we move from the study to the pulpit.

Perhaps a word concerning the preacher's motive is in order. Some preachers become so passionate about the content of a sermon that they will preach it regardless of the congregation. This motive has merit. It places a high premium on the divine aspect of the sermon. To the preacher, the sermon comes from God. The preacher's duty is discharged in its proclamation.

Others preach to connect the Word of God to the lives of the hearers. For this type of preacher, the congregation is of primary concern. They study the potential congregation and gauge the impact and effect of the sermon on lives as they understand them. The first type of preacher sees the work as finished with the proclamation itself. The second sees the work as done only when hearing that leads to understanding has occurred.

If one looks at the congregation as made up of individuals who have given a precious gift to the preacher, the second type appears more appropriate. In fact, the congregation *has* given a gift to the preacher – time, time that could have been spent in any number of ways. They have chosen to set that time aside to hear a word from God. That fact alone dictates the place the congregation should hold in the preacher's mind.

Every word counts. John Stott calculated, "If we preach only once a week for forty years, we shall utter about nine million [words]."[19] Certainly words matter, for they are the basic element of our craft. Selecting and arranging those words reflects the skill level of the preacher. This step starts with the development of an outline. With the two basic sentences in hand (essence of the text and essence of the sermon), the preacher begins to construct a skeleton, or outline, for the sermon. The outline takes the sermon from its one-sentence essence and frames it to full length. Each point of the outline must connect back to that one sentence, stating the heart of the sermon while remaining consistent with the text. There is no best number of points, nor is there any one way of developing them.

The ethical content determined from the text can constitute the points of the outline. In another sermon, the ethical content of the text can be considered in one of the points but not all of them – these other points would develop other aspects of the text. Still another sermon might hold the ethical content back for the application, which might appear as the conclusion. It is not necessary to have every point and its development be a consideration of the ethical position of the text in order to have the sermon address ethical issues. Nor is it proper to force an ethical position on the text. Our call for a strengthening of ethical preaching is a call to authentic proclamation; it is not license for the preacher to take off on a personal tangent. The Bible is filled with possibilities for ethical preaching; there is no reason to abuse Scripture for that purpose.

The place to start for the preacher is in determining how the text selected for the sermon speaks ethically, to the extent that it does do so. We believe the place to begin is with the model offered in chapter 2. First, the text may offer an ethical-theological stance, vision, or framework – for example, a text dealing with the nature of God or of the church. Such texts will generally be broad in scope. No one sermon will adequately speak to every point that could be made of a text containing such a significant ethical-theological stance. So the preacher might consider turning this ethical truth around, examining different facets of the truth as the different major divisions within the sermon, and then taking a different tack the next time that text is considered.

Some texts are more specific. They contain ethical principles that are more pointed and limited in scope. For instance, 2 Corinthians 5:19, "God was reconciling the world to himself in Christ, not counting men's sins against them," is a clear statement concerning the character and activity of God (theological-ethical framework level), but it both has implicit ethical implications and flows directly into a statement with implications at the principle level: "We are therefore Christ's ambassadors, as though God were making his appeal through us" (v. 20). This two-verse statement opens the door for a variety of ethically oriented sermonic approaches. The points could turn on different facets of the work of reconciliation or they could build on each other, telescoping out from the text to daily application. The preacher is not limited except by his or her own abilities.

Some texts offer us concrete rules for daily life and practice. Those rules can be stated in either negative or positive
ways with benefit to the hearers. It is possible to see Paul's
admonishment to avoid being "yoked together with unbeliev-
ers" (2 Corinthians 6:14) as a negative articulation of an ethical
rule. However, it can be preached for great benefit to individual
Christians in need of assistance as they build their interpersonal
relationships. On the other hand, Jesus' command to "love each
other as I have loved you" (John 15:12) is a positively stated
rule even though it can restrict the actions of Christians in their
congregational life. The preacher should perhaps exercise more
care at this level (rules) than any other, because this level of
ethical preaching, while of great value and importance, opens
up the potential of an unhelpful legalism.

The final development of ethical preaching is at the point
of direct application to the life situation of the congregation.
Some texts, such as James 1:27, simply cry out for specific ethical responses. Here the apostle James teaches that authentic
religion is ethical, and he names caring for widows and orphans
in their distress as obligatory. Thus, the text might establish the
movement of the sermon depending on the way in which the
ethical content is offered. In this case, the text demands direct
reflection by the preacher on the ways in which the congregation is living out, or failing to live out, the meaning of this
passage.

When the outline is formed, the preacher can build on its
points. This is accomplished by the careful choice of words,
for words constitute the flesh of the outline's skeleton, both as
the expansion of the points and as illustrations used to illuminate the points. Putting these different components together is
the task of the preacher. When done properly the text comes
alive – the sermon's essence penetrates the heart, and an ethical truth is delivered there. Thus, the minister moves to the final
preaching responsibility – providing the congregation with a
balanced diet of such well-delivered truths over a sustained
period of time.

The preacher is not allowed much time to mourn sermon
failures or applaud pulpit successes; there is always a Sunday
coming. Indeed, the burnout factor among ministers is so high

in part because of the constant pressure to preach. There are no real shortcuts to preparation, though many seek them. Each sermon makes genuine demands on the preacher's time, effort, and energy. The wise preacher builds a system to maximize his resources. As we have stated before, there is no single best system. Some preachers work with the lectionary. Some preachers preach systematically, book by book, through the Bible. Others work off a theme established for a period of time – a quarter, half, or full year. A helpful hint to remember is the longer the period of time the simpler the theme. A simple theme allows the preacher room to move across the year while exploring the many facets of that theme. Our preference obviously would be for a system that makes room for a sustained treatment of the moral questions raised by particular biblical texts or themes. Meanwhile, the preacher needs to be flexible enough to step away from the schedule in order to provide God's word for that moment. It is important to review periodically one's repertoire of sermon offerings over the past quarter, year, or decade. Test these for ethical content and, of course, for overall balance and fidelity to the canon of Scripture and the needs of God's people.

Conclusion

We began with a complaint: There is a moral vacuum in much of today's preaching that has had negative effects on American Christianity as well as society at large. Yet it can be addressed and changed. In chapter 2 we offered a grid for reading Scripture and for thinking about the moral dimension of the gospel. In this chapter we considered the character of the preacher and turned to the practical matter of building a model for ethically sensitive preaching. Now we turn our attention to the task of considering individual texts and themes for their preaching possibilities.

NOTES

1. John R. W. Stott, *Between Two Worlds: The Art of Preaching in the Twentieth Century* (Grand Rapids: Eerdmans, 1982), 138.

2. Phillips Brooks, *Lectures on Preaching* (Grand Rapids: Baker, 1907; reprint 1969), 5.

3. James Ward and Christine Ward, *Preaching from the Prophets* (Nashville: Abingdon, 1995), 15.

4. Halford Luccock, *In the Minister's Workshop* (Nashville: Abingdon-Cokesbury, 1944), 149.

5. John A. Broadus, *On the Preparation and Delivery of Sermons*, 4th ed. (Harper and Row, 1979), 16.

6. Ibid.

7. Paramount Studios, *Teacher's Pet*, 1958.

8. Stott, *Between Two Worlds*, 182.

9. Harold Bryson and James C. Taylor, *Building Sermons to Meet People's Needs* (Nashville: Broadman, 1980), 9.

10. James F. Childress and John Macquarrie, eds., *The Westminster Dictionary of Christian Ethics* (Philadelphia: Westminster, 1986). Compare the newer and more conservative *New Dictionary of Christian Ethics and Pastoral Theology* (Downers Grove, Ill.: InterVarsity Press, 1995).

11. U.S. Bureau of the Census, *Statistical Abstract of the United States* (Washington, D.C.). To obtain a copy, contact the National Technical Information Service (Springfield, Va.) or the Census Bureau. A new edition is published each year.

12. In Broadus, *Preparation and Delivery of Sermons*, 54.

13. Ibid., 58.

14. James Stewart, *The Heralds of God* (New York: Charles Scribner's Sons, 1946), 109.

15. In Broadus, *Preparation and Delivery of Sermons*, 58.

16. Paul Scherer, *For We Have This Treasure* (New York: Harper, 1944), 165.

17. Harold Bryson, *Expository Preaching* (Nashville: Broadman and Holman, 1995), 34.

18. Bryson and Taylor, *Building Sermons*, 9.

19. Stott, *Between Two Worlds*, 231.

Part 2

SERMONS

A Steward in Every Sense

Genesis 1

This Sunday evening sermon, preached in early 1998 at Walnut Street, focused on the environment through an exposition of passages in Genesis 1. It is striking how significant the early chapters of Genesis are for both Christian theology and ethics, and that is no-where truer than on the subject of the environment. This sermon attempts to move through conservative Christian opposition to the extremes of the secular environmental movement toward a healthy, biblical Christian approach. It is brush-clearing work, one might say, focusing on the theological framework level and not attempting to offer specific policy prescriptions. — rhl

Introduction

Please take your Bibles and open them to the book of Genesis, the book of beginnings. The great theologian Karl Barth suggested that the best way Christians could approach life would be to have a Bible in one hand and a newspaper in the other. In the weeks ahead, we will look at some of the issues that perplex and challenge us. I hope to cause us to think through critically what it means to be a Christian. Tonight our topic is the environment.

The first verse of Scripture begins with God the Creator intensely engaged in shaping what we call the environment but is in fact God's creation.

In the beginning God created the heavens and the earth. Now
the earth was formless and empty, darkness was over the surface
of the deep, and the Spirit of God was hovering over the waters.
    And God said, "Let there be light," and there was light. God
saw that the light was good, and he separated the light from the
darkness. God called the light "day," and the darkness he called
"night." And there was evening, and there was morning – the
first day.

You can go on and read through the rest of the creation
story on your own. I want us to skip down to the last phrase
of verse 25: "And God saw that it was good." This summary
statement is used seven times in the early portions of Genesis
to describe what the biblical account has to say about God's
work in creating the world. God saw that it was good. Verses
26 through 30 say:

Then God said, 'Let us make man in our image, in our likeness,
and let them rule over the fish of the sea and the birds of the air,
over the livestock, over all the earth, and over all the creatures
that move along the ground."

So God created man in his own image,
    in the image of God he created him;
    male and female he created them.

God blessed them and said to them, "Be fruitful and increase in
number; fill the earth and subdue it. Rule over the fish of the sea
and the birds of the air and over every living creature that moves
on the ground."
    Then God said, "I give you every seed-bearing plant on the
face of the whole earth and every tree that has fruit with seed
in it. They will be yours for food. And to all the beasts of the
earth and all the birds of the air and all the creatures that move
on the ground – everything that has breath of life in it – I give
every green plant for food." And it was so.

Then the summary verse of the entire chapter:

God saw all that he had made, and it was very good. And there
was evening, and there was morning – the sixth day.

I must confess that my earliest contact with a committed en-
vironmentalist was a distasteful experience to say the least. He
was a Greenpeace activist. Greenpeace is a highly controversial
environmental group. And, to make matters worse, he had in-
terrupted my dinner. There are certain things that you eat only

on occasions where you really have a taste for them. Fried fish, for me, is one of those dishes. The meal had been prepared. I knew that I was going to have to endure the smell of cooked fish in the house all evening. I wanted to enjoy my dinner, and yet this guy was on my porch talking to me about Mother Earth and our responsibility to take care of Mother as she provides life for us. Before the evening was over, he and I got into a rather intense discussion. At that time, I just dismissed him as a zealot. But I have learned much since then. It was very possible that he represented the extremes of one end of the spectrum. I hate to admit it – indeed, I am not quite ready to admit it yet – but it may very well be that, at the time, I represented the other extreme of the same spectrum.

I will not soon forget my conversation with my adversary. As we stood on my porch, he told me about some of the activities of Greenpeace. He said that if I were a conscientious person, a person of character and ethics, I should contribute to his cause. I talked to him about the illegality of his cause. His was the zealot's answer that when humans make laws only to perpetuate their greed and destroy Mother Earth, then you and I are not bound to heed them. I told him that I was not sure I was a part of Mother Earth. I didn't quite buy into that philosophy. I explained that I had a more theocentric opinion about how the earth came into being. In one motion, this young activist dismissed theology by saying that any notion of God, even if God did exist, was highly subjective. For me, talking about God is not nearly as subjective as talking about Mother Earth. And it is not nearly as offensive to me as talking about Mother Earth.

I have discovered that there are those in our world who look at the earth as a masterpiece while seeking to dismiss the Master who made it. That is dangerous, because one of two things will happen if you take that view. You will eventually elevate the masterpiece itself to the level of the Creator or you will simply exploit all that it has to offer.

It has been suggested, and I think it is correct, that the only person capable of truly appreciating the earth for what it is, is a Christian. That may be a controversial thought. However, I think it is very true. At the time of my conversation with the man from Greenpeace, I probably represented too much of the other extreme of the spectrum, which was to be unconcerned about the world and its resources. But I have since discovered that there are a lot of things Christians should be concerned about environmentally. We should be concerned that humans exploit, that we rip out, tear away, and destroy, and we have no mechanism in place for putting back. Those who dismiss God in favor of their economic advancement, their financial status, their claims to their world end up exploiting the resources of the earth and destroying the environment.

Three words seem to frame biblical thought concerning the environment. Let's examine them together. The first word is *authority*. The second is *priority*. And the third is *responsibility*. If you and I are going to talk about what the Bible has to say about the earth, about the environment, then we should begin by understanding that the Bible assigns all life to the authority of God. In the beginning God created – what a wonderful thought. In fact, I want us to go back and focus on these first two verses. "In the beginning God created the heavens and the earth. Now the earth was formless and empty, darkness was over the surface of the deep, and the Spirit of God was thundering [perhaps a better translation] over the waters." Storming across the face of the waters. The Bible seems to say that God *appoints, orders*, and *names* all creation.

It is very interesting that we would be able to single out those activities – God names all that he creates, identifies it, and then begins to catalog it for us. Those are essentially the functions of a sovereign. In biblical times a sovereign had the right to name, the responsibility to name, and the authority to name. From the very beginning, the Bible makes a very specific claim about the environment. Creation is God's. If we fail to recognize God's role in creating the world, we create for ourselves all kinds of trouble. We see our world as a wonderful masterpiece while leaving out any thought of the Master by whose hands it was created. Thus, we eventually deify the masterpiece and dismiss as inconsequential the Master. But creation is God's.

The Bible goes on to say a couple of other things about God's authority in relation to creation. It says that the earth, like so much else that God has made, is itself a part of how we come to understand God. It is as though God has made the world to resemble himself. Now, that does not mean that the world around us is a form of God. That is a heresy, and we need to be very careful that we not fall into that kind of vocabulary. It means that what God made from the very beginning informs us about God. In the same way that you come to know an author as you read a book that he or she has written, you come to know something about God as you see his handiwork. When we see what God has done in the world, in creation, we begin to sense that God is a God of profound beauty. Our God is a God of wonderful mystery and power, and yet all that he has made seems to work in harmony. There is a beauty about it. But tragically, the Bible makes another very straightforward claim. Sin, when it is introduced into the human condition, mars that which holds God's image. It mars everything. Sin is like ugly goo that sticks on a shoreline somewhere. Everything that touches it is fouled by it. Sin marred the world, the environment, in the same way sin marred humankind and our relationship with God.

This leads us to the third point about God's authority and the environment. God's intention has always been not just to redeem humanity but to redeem everything that sin stained. Everything that sin rotted, everything that sin mired, everything that sin distorted, God is ultimately going to reclaim. The book of Revelation is a very difficult book to understand, but one of its more straightforward points is near the end, where John, the one to whom all of this is revealed, says, "I saw a new heaven and a new earth, for the first heaven and the first earth had passed away" (21:1). Ultimately God is going to restore everything that sin has distorted, and that includes the environment.

But it doesn't stop there. Scripture also talks about a priority in created order. That priority rests with its apex at the creation of humanity. Look again at Genesis 1:27. It may not be something secular environmentalists would like to hear, but it is the biblical relationship in creation.

> God created man in his own image,
> in the image of God he created him;
> male and female he created them.

Humankind is the top of the heap of God's creation. Some people want to talk about how we are equal with other forms of creation. But talking about other forms of creation as though they are elevated to the same level as humanity is to dismiss the biblical point that God has created with a sense of priority. If we don't understand that God has created with a sense of priority, we can easily dismiss the fact that God has created at all. I think we are going to have to come back and understand that God created a world where humans are at the apex of created order, without diminishing the real value of all other forms of created life.

The Bible goes even further. It talks about the world being under human dominion. Probably none of the English words we have used really captures the essence of what God has done. God has created a hierarchy of responsibility and privilege. Those two work together. God has not given us freedom to act indiscriminately in the natural world. You will notice as you read this passage of Scripture that originally there were very careful outlines of where and how human beings could exercise dominion. For instance, humans had dominion in the sense that we could eat any of the plants that fell into the categories God established. But not animals. It seems to be that our lust for a good piece of beef comes because of our fall into sin. That's okay. I'm not expecting to discover that we become a bunch of vegetarians as a result of tonight's sermon. But I am suggesting to you that from the very beginning when God allowed humanity to be at the apex of creation, our role has been to exercise that priority responsibly.

This leads me to the last word, *responsibility*. We are stewards — not owners. To be a steward means the world is not ours to do with as we see fit. We are responsible not solely to ourselves or our neighbors but ultimately to God for how we act and the impact our decisions have on others, some of whom have yet to be born. We should take seriously every destruction that comes to the environment. I do not have the right to extract what I want and to leave the rest behind. I don't have the right to exploit. We have responsibilities as stewards to manage the resources of God's world in such a way that they are preserved and passed on to others yet unborn.

So many times we come to the conclusion that what is good for industry must be God's will. We always seem willing to sacrifice creation for profit. Every time we're confronted with an issue of whether we ought to do something that is economically beneficial or something that preserves a sense of the texture of this world in its natural condition, it is not the right Christian answer simply to develop. We salve our conscience by thinking that we ought to develop carefully and we ought to develop responsibly, but we ought always to develop. No, we ought not always develop. Because to destroy all that is natural is to diminish and tear away a part of the face of God that is painted on the canvas of the earth. We are not good stewards when we lightly allow that to happen and dismiss it as though it has no consequence.

What about the Christian and the environment? Well, there will always be extremists who seem to elevate the environment inappropriately. I am not asking you to do that, but I am asking you to take seriously the fact that we are stewards of God's creation over which he has authority, and responsibility, which he has entrusted into our hands. There is much more to be said and much more to be done, but here is where we begin.

The Sanctity of Human Life
Genesis 1:26–27

This sermon was the first I preached at Northbrook Church, the seeker-oriented congregation in which I now serve. Northbrook includes numerous non-Christians, believers from other faith traditions, and new Christians. This helps to explain the effort in this sermon to define terms that might be assumed in other church contexts. The sermon takes a thematic approach to the principle of the sanctity of human life, based on Genesis 1:26–27 and other texts, and essentially works at the theological framework and broad moral principle levels. It does include more brief, concrete applications to a range of contemporary moral issues. Among the issues that receive brief mention is the particularly controversial and emotional topic of abortion. Intelligent and committed Christians disagree on various aspects of the abortion issue, and the stance represented here is not universally shared in the Christian community. I offer my own conviction on this and other sensitive issues without apology but with respect for those who differ. — dpg

Introduction: The Moral Dimension of Christian Faith

The Christian faith has many dimensions and elements, doesn't it? We have many things to learn if we are serious about Christianity.

- We need to learn about how to have a relationship with God and then how to continue in that relationship once it starts. Let's call this the *spiritual* dimension of Christian faith.

- We need to learn what to believe about God, Jesus, the Holy Spirit, the world, sin, death, and so on. This is the *doctrinal* dimension of Christian faith.

- We need to learn about what the church is supposed to be, how it works, what membership means, what our mission is, how we are to relate to one another, and so much more. Let's call this the *ecclesial* dimension of Christian faith.

- There is one other area of the Christian faith that we need to learn about. We need to learn how to apply the teachings of Scripture to every area of our daily lives. We also need to know how to apply Scripture to the world we live in, how to make our lives intersect the way they should with the world, society, culture, and even law and government. This final area we'll call the *moral* or ethical dimension of Christian faith.

It's this last area that I want to talk with you about tonight. Why? Well, one reason is that dealing with this whole moral dimension of Christianity is what I do all day. I am trained in Christian ethics and teach it at Union University. So I love this subject. I'm biased – I admit it.

But the other reason is much more important. I think that the moral dimension of the faith is both the most neglected, on the one hand, and the most abused, on the other, in the church today. It is neglected in that many churches do not seem to have Christian morality on their agenda. They shy away from anything that gets in the ballpark. They're looking at moral problems in their midst and moral chaos in society, and they say nothing.

This is happening because of both a history and a current reality of abuse in this area of concern. Many people today who went to church as kids grew up dealing with a real tight, strict, repressive legalism in church. Christian morality was about telling you all the things you were not supposed to do, like wear blue jeans to church, or dance, or wear makeup.

Today the problem is not so much legalism but politicization. Many of the moral issues that we care about the most, and rightly so, have been taken into the political arena. There they have been handled in such a divisive and often cynical way

that we'd rather never hear them discussed in church. When issues like abortion or homosexuality become political footballs,
it becomes hard to step back and think about them with a clear
Christian mind and heart. This is the backlash effect.

But you see, we don't really have that choice. If our goal is to
be the kind of Christians God wants us to be, we must subject
every area of life to scriptural scrutiny and direction. This includes morality – both our most private decisions and lifestyles
and the most public moral issues of our day. Tonight I would
simply like to lay the foundation for an overall approach to the
moral dimension of the faith.

Sanctity of Human Life: Theological Basics

The single phrase that I think best communicates the heart of
the Christian moral life is "the sanctity of human life." Some
of you will be quite familiar with this term; others of you may
never have heard of it.

Instead of just defining it here, let's look at three theological
basics that together point to what this term means. First, *God
is the author of human life*. Let's read Genesis 2:7: "The LORD
God formed the man from the dust of the ground and breathed
into his nostrils the breath of life, and the man became a living
being."

The Bible tells us that God was directly and personally responsible for making the first man, Adam, and the first woman,
Eve. God formed Adam out of the dust of the ground. What a
wonderful and rich image.

But it's not like he stopped there. The Scripture repeatedly
celebrates God's authorship of human life. Hear these words
from Psalm 139:

> For you created my inmost being;
>   you knit me together in my mother's womb.
> I praise you because I am fearfully and wonderfully made;
>   your works are wonderful,
>   I know that full well.
> My frame was not hidden from you
>   when I was made in the secret place.

> When I was woven together in the depths of the earth,
>   your eyes saw my unformed body.
> All the days ordained for me
>   were written in your book
>   before one of them came to be. (vv. 13-16)

Many people today think that the entire planet is a cosmic accident and human life a very interesting coincidence. You know — some cosmic soup, some bacteria, and boom, a couple of billion years later you've got Mozart. But the Bible affirms that we exist by God's will, that we are the creatures of a loving creator God.

Second, *God made us "in his image" and "likeness."* Let's read Genesis 1:26-27:

> Then God said, "Let us make man in our image, in our likeness, and let them rule over the fish of the sea and the birds of the air, over the livestock, over all the earth, and over all the creatures that move along the ground."
>
> > So God created man in his own image,
> >   in the image of God he created him;
> >   male and female he created them.

To be made in the image of God means two things. One has to do with the attributes that we share in common with God. Our capacities reflect his — things like our ability to think, to love, to relate to people, to make choices. God made us in these ways like himself. How remarkable that we were designed to share certain attributes of God our Maker.

The other has to do not with human attributes but with responsibilities. To be made in the image of God is to share in the tasks of God, the work of God on this earth. We will "image" God — represent God — to the rest of creation. We see this already in this passage, where God commands us to take responsibility and represent his rule over the fish, birds, livestock, and all other creatures.

Third, *God has declared human life worthy of honor, glory, and respect.* Psalm 8:3-5 says:

> > When I consider your heavens,
> >   the work of your fingers,
> > the moon and the stars,
> >   which you have set in place,

> what is man that you are mindful of him,
>   the son of man that you care for him?
> You made him a little lower than the heavenly beings
>   and crowned him with glory and honor.

Despite our many obvious faults and our deeply embedded sinful nature, God has crowned humanity as a whole, and each human life in particular, with glory and honor. We are declared to be just "a little lower than the heavenly beings" – some translations say, "than God himself."

So, what have we seen so far? God is the author of every human life. God made us in his image, his likeness. God has declared human life worthy of honor, glory, and respect. These are the theological truths that undergird the concept of the "sanctity of human life."

To speak of the sanctity of human life is to claim that God has declared both by action and by his Word that every human life is of immense value to him. *Sanctity* comes from the Latin *sanctus*, which means holy. Christians believe that God has declared every human life sacred, holy, not because of our own moral goodness but because of the value that he himself has placed upon it. God sees each of us as special, set apart, not to be trifled with, dishonored, or disrespected. Perhaps the highest way to say it is this: God loves us.

Sanctity of Human Life: Moral Implications

This immense value that God places on our lives has tremendous moral implications, both for individual life and broader social and moral issues. Let's look at a couple of basic moral implications of this theological truth and then move to some contemporary applications.

First moral implication: *We must value human lives according to God's standard, not our own.* Listen to James 2:1–4:

My brothers, as believers in our glorious Lord Jesus Christ, don't show favoritism. Suppose a man comes into your meeting wearing a gold ring and fine clothes, and a poor man in shabby clothes also comes in. If you show special attention to the man wearing fine clothes and say, "Here's a good seat for you," but say to the poor man, "You stand there" or "Sit on the floor by my feet," have you not discriminated among yourselves and become judges with evil thoughts?

If God sees human beings as of extraordinary importance, we must as well. If God loves people, we must too. We tend to love only a handful of people, those closest to us. But that is the way that God loves everyone, and much more. We must learn to value and to love with God's standards. It doesn't matter how "useful" a person is, or how attractive, how young, how old, how intelligent, or anything else – God bestows value on each life, and that value remains constant from conception until death. We are to treat each other accordingly. And that attitude will carry over into our public witness.

Second moral implication: *We must work to prevent violence and other assaults on the sanctity of human life*. Exodus 20:13 says, "You shall not murder." The sixth commandment is a critical part of the sanctity of human life. The sacredness of human life implies reverence for life at every stage from conception to death. It implies that the right to life is the first and fundamental human right. It requires that believing Christians be on the front lines of efforts to end the shedding of human blood wherever it occurs.

Please try to feel how much God detests violence, the shedding of each other's blood that we do. God made us for better than this, and the sacredness of our lives implies, indeed demands, that we refrain from killing each other and that we act to prevent the killing of others. Third moral implication: *We must cherish and seek the flourishing of each other's lives*. Matthew 22:39 reads, "Love your neighbor as yourself." The sacredness of human life means not only that we refrain from killing each other (a negative prohibition), but that we take positive steps to cherish each other. We are called to do everything we can to contribute to the flourishing of every human life. I think that this is fundamentally what is meant when we are called to "love one another" or to "love our neighbor as ourselves." Can you imagine how different the world would look if the church was busy doing this? How different the church itself would look?

Sanctity of Human Life:
Contemporary Applications

Properly understood, the sanctity of human life is a life-changing concept. It will cause you to look at the world around you – from your most immediate relationships to the most dramatic global events – and see things differently. Actually, you'll see *people* differently, and you'll treat people differently – because you'll know in your heart and soul that this person I'm dealing with today, or this person I'm watching suffer on television, is sacred before God.

Let's close this evening by bowing our heads in prayer and lifting up before God eight areas of concern about the sacredness of human life. As I name these, reflect for a moment on the issue involved and, if you are willing, silently join me in prayer.

1. Personal Relationships

Here we think about our friends and family, those people with whom God intends that we should experience life's sanctity most profoundly. Yet family life is so badly marred – by cruelty; verbal abuse; physical abuse; even murder.

O Lord, help us to treat those closest to us as if they are sacred before you.

2. Sexuality

When expressed properly and in the context of marriage, this is an aspect of life in which sanctity is profoundly experienced. But it is also violated in so many ways: sexual exploitation, rape, objectifying persons rather than valuing them. We must oppose any reduction of people into objects for our pleasure. Sex is neither entertainment nor mere recreation.

O Lord, help us to treat all members of the opposite sex as if they are sacred before you.

3. Race

The principle of the sanctity of life insists on universal application. All are made in the image of God; all life is sacred. Racism contradicts the sanctity of life by placing full value only on *some* lives. We think of Nazi racism, the racism in our own country, or that which can be found all over the world. We must oppose any "racialized" scheme for looking at people.

O Lord, help us to treat people of other races as if they are sacred before you.

4. Poverty and hunger

God intends that all human beings should have their basic needs met. On the one hand, it's part of the right to life, and on the other, it has to do with God's intended flourishing of all lives. So when a child (or anyone) dies of starvation, God grieves. He grieves because that person was sacred and God intended so much more. On a smaller scale, the same is true of a grinding poverty that does not kill but does utterly degrade. We must oppose any "lifeboat ethic" or any lack of caring for "the least of these."

O Lord, help us to treat the hungry of our nation and the world as sacred before you.

5. Genocide

The right to life for all people and groups obviously forbids mass murder of one group of people by another. Yet that is exactly what has happened now more than once in this century — the Armenian genocide in 1917–18, the Holocaust, the killings by Pol Pot in Cambodia, and mass slaughter in Uganda, Rwanda, and Bosnia. Those rulers and nations that commit genocide have strayed unimaginably far from the concept of the sanctity of life.

O Lord, we grieve these tragedies. Help us to treat the victimized of the world as sacred before you.

6. War

Human history is full of wars, but the Christian tradition insists that God's intention is peace; that war is profound evidence of human sinfulness; that Christians are called to be peacemakers; and that the only legitimate war is a genuinely defensive one. We must oppose any view that sees war as a legitimate tool for just getting what a nation wants. Life is too sacred for that view to hold.

O Lord, free us from a warlike spirit. Help us to know that our nation's enemies are sacred before you.

7. Suicide/Euthanasia

Two years ago the people of Oregon passed a referendum allowing physician-assisted suicide for the first time. Two federal appeals courts have affirmed such a right. Imagine authorizing doctors to help their patients kill themselves! Christians who understand the sanctity of life can only shudder.

O Lord, help us to treat the very ill, the very old, and the dying as sacred before you.

8. Abortion

Roughly 1.3 million pregnancies are ended every year by abortion in the United States. Many circumstances drive people into this decision. But your Word gives us no reason to think that the life of the unborn child is less sacred to you than any other life. Nevertheless, for now, our nation has permitted legalized abortion. And so it continues.

O Lord, help us to treat the unborn children and their mothers as sacred before you. O Lord, for Northbrook Church, I pray for your wisdom and guidance concerning how we as a body are to bring biblical moral convictions into our life and our witness. How we need your guidance. Bless us as a body and as individuals and families tonight as we seek to treat others as sacred in your sight. Amen.

Down and Out
on Market Street
Genesis 4:1–12

Walnut Street Baptist Church has deliberately chosen to stay in downtown Louisville. The cost for such a choice is high for any congregation. Occasionally the pulpit becomes the launching pad for an apologetic to the entire congregation on the rationale for staying. August 1995's theme was "Strong Ties to the City We Call Home." It explores the Cain and Abel story as a way to remake the case for staying in the city, which is one of the most important moral practices our entire church has ever undertaken. This is clearly a sermon addressed to a particular local congregation as a body, yet it has personal implications for all who read and hear it. — rhl

I'd like to share with you a story that was reported on the sports page of the Jacksonville, Florida, newspaper last Sunday. It is a story about a man named Paul Shirley who is an orthopedic surgeon in Jacksonville and is also a partner in an enterprise called Blue Water International, a group of individuals – I suspect many of them are doctors – who go into Central America and lead tourist excursions up and down some of the navigable waters there. They take them to see a part of the world that you and I don't see every day.

On July 1 of this year – it was a Saturday – Dr. Shirley was on the San Juan River on the sixty-five-foot houseboat his company owns. The San Juan is the river that separates Nicaragua from Costa Rica. He and a fellow doctor, Alfredo Lopez, a Central American, decided they would stop and take about a six-

97

or eight-hour excursion up into the jungle region to carve out a trail where they could take the more adventurous of their clients later on. They decided they would spend a night blazing this trail in the wilderness, a part of the world where very few human beings ever go. They took enough provisions for their overnight adventure, but after the first night, with the rains of the jungle and the water and the humidity, they knew they had some problems. Moisture had gotten into the electronic tracking device that allowed them to send a signal to the outside world to let people know where they were. So now they were in this jungle and all alone.

To make matters worse, sometime in the second day of the journey they ran out of all of the fluids that they had taken with them to drink. They had nothing to eat and nothing to drink but the polluted water of the jungle streams. Going through one of the swamps just on the other side of a mountain range they had already crossed, Dr. Shirley experienced what you and I would think would be an inconvenience but in the jungle is a pretty serious problem. In the muck and mire of the jungle, he lost the heel from one of his boots. He was beginning to get sick from the water he had been forced to drink, and now his shoe was coming apart. There was no food. They had already killed one snake, a very dangerous poisonous snake, just inches before the snake would have sunk its fangs into Dr. Lopez. And even though Dr. Lopez was also sick, it was agreed that Dr. Lopez would take the one machete and a compass and see if he could make his way back to the river. As they talked together, both of them realized that if Dr. Lopez lost his way and didn't get back in time, Dr. Shirley would die in that jungle.

Eventually, Dr. Shirley recognized that if he were to survive at all, he would have to eat something; so taking the mosquito netting, he began to seine a little pool of water for minnows. He was forced to eat them alive and then to continue drinking the water from the polluted streams. Nausea was beginning to overwhelm him. He lapsed in and out of a delirium. After a while, his eyes absorbed so much moisture that his cornea had a yellowish ring around it, so he saw everything through a yellowish haze surrounded by a ring. He thought he was going to die. He saved one bullet for his rifle because the last thing he consciously thought was, "I don't want to feel what it is like to be eaten alive." He had a disposable camera, the kind you throw away after the film is gone. He took a picture of himself in the jungle and hoped it would survive so that his children would have a last remembrance of him should he ever be found. On Thursday of that week, through the haze, three men approached him. They were fishermen he had used at different times. They guided him back through the river streams and eventually brought him back to the river and his houseboat.

What was so amazing to him, and what I found so amazing about the story, was that he looked out on that river and there was a flotilla of fishing boats. All the fishermen who lived on the river had been out searching for him and Dr. Lopez. Not only that, he found out later that the American Embassy was just about to send troops into the region, with those governments' approval, to start searching for him. Most amazing still was that a Nicaraguan general had allowed his troops to go over into Costa Rica and had also allowed Costa Rican troops into Nicaragua. This was something that no one had ever heard of before. It just was not supposed to happen. But it did.

I asked myself, why would people go to such lengths to look for someone? Why would they care so much? The story included some clues. Not only did the doctors take tourists up and down those rivers, but everywhere they went, they left medicine, food, clothing, and toys for the children of the river valley inhabitants. Everywhere they went, they took a little touch of grace and gave it to other people. I would like to be able to report to you that this doctor is an outstanding Christian. But I don't know. I don't know if he claims to know Jesus Christ as his Lord. I don't know if he even cares. But I do know this: He gave more of a demonstration of grace than a lot of churches I know ever do. If he is not a Christian, it is to our undying shame that he reflects more of God's goodness than we sometimes do.

We live in a time in which we in the church, unfortunately, spend more time arguing about what we think about the Bible than putting any of it into practice. So we walk around and pretend that the ones we do not care about do not exist rather than stooping over and helping. Then we wonder why it is the world doesn't even bother to check inside our doors to see if perhaps there is some truth in what we proclaim. We have a huge, thick alligator hide of Phariseeism never pricked by the love of Christ.

I talked a few years ago to an official of the Home Mission Board of our Southern Baptist Convention. I had just come to be your pastor. We were talking about Walnut Street and its unique heritage and wonderful history, not only in this city but beyond. He asked me the obvious question: "Are you going to stay?" I knew exactly what he meant. He meant, "Are you going to stay here on this corner and minister here in the name of the Lord in this place and be the only Jesus that some of the folks of the city of Louisville will ever see?" I said, "Yes. I can't speak for the church, but I believe in my heart that we are going to stay." He said, "Thank God. We Baptists and others have left our cities, boarded our buildings, and sold our property — if God gives us a future, we are going to have to go back, because we cannot leave our cities without a voice. We can't just leave."

You see, in our society, we don't move those whom we don't want to see outside the city limits. We move ourselves to areas where we no longer have to look at the things we don't like to see. In the pages of our history, I see the same question that is posed for us at the dawn of life. Who is responsible?

You turn four pages into the text of the Bible. In my Bible Genesis 4 is on page 4. You turn four pages into the history of who we are, and you begin to see that the corrosive effect of sin is beginning to make some awful, hideous changes in what it is like to be a human being. Before sin intervened and caused humans to sever the life-giving relationship they had with God, I believe they lived in a world whose atmosphere was drenched in grace. It was as natural for people then to live in a world filled with grace as it is natural for us now to live in a world filled with air. But what happened when sin severed the relationship that human beings had with God is that we lost, as a consequence, our ability to live in a world filled with grace. Wouldn't it be a grand thing if we lived in a world so touched by the presence of God that grace surrounded us just like air does? If we lived in a world where we wouldn't have to see brief glimpses of God's grace but would see and live and breathe the very presence of God's grace?

But in four pages life has been radically changed. This is a very complex passage of Scripture, this fourth chapter of Genesis, the story of Cain and Abel. There are all kinds of lessons we can learn from this passage. It doesn't take long for the human condition to get so out of balance that instead of caring for and nurturing and helping one another, we turn our backs and pretend that others don't even exist. That is what happens here. The Bible doesn't really explicitly say why it is that God is not pleased with the offering that Cain brings. Down through history, a lot of theologians and preachers alike have supposed that it is because Cain brought a pitiful offering. Perhaps he just brought a little something, a little piddling offering that indicated that he didn't really have much respect or much love for God, but actually it is quite likely that Cain brought a very good offering. What Cain didn't do was to bring the best offering.

Abel did. The first fruits. Throughout the Old Testament the first fruits are considered the best fruits. It is as if Cain brought an offering that said, "God, thanks for being my silent partner. Thanks for sending rain and sunshine in just the right amounts and allowing me to produce this great crop. Thanks for being there when I wanted you to be there." But Abel brought an offering that suggested that he understood he was totally dependent upon the God of the universe to sustain his life. Cain brought an offering that said, "God I am glad you were there for me." Abel brought an offering that said, "God, I know that I can't live without you." Cain brought an offering that said, "God, let's do it again next year." Abel brought an offering that said, "God, I need you every hour."

We know that Cain had a problem with his attitude where God is concerned, because when the Bible says God turned down Cain's offering, Cain's attitude was reflected in his face. His face became a mirror to his heart. And his heart was cold and empty, his face downcast. He took his brother, Abel, out into a field and killed him. God talked to him there. "What have you done, Cain?" Cain's arrogant answer has been the answer of humanity for centuries. Looking in the face of God, he says, "God, I am not responsible. If I have been given much, that is just because I have worked hard. If I am blessed, I deserve it. But don't you go blaming me, God, and don't you go telling me that I am responsible."

The church down through its history has had the same struggle. We have dealt with the same question. Who is responsible? Part of the time we will throw a little bit of something in the direction of those in need and briefly feel better. Many times we just simply say it is not our task. But it is. The Lord says to us that we are connected. If there is hopelessness in the world and an absence of grace, it is because you and I have not put the grace into place where others could see some hope. Our Lord says to us, "Who is responsible?"

There was a day in the life of Jesus when a student of the Law came and said to Jesus, "How can I have eternal life?" You and I might phrase the question this way – "How can I have grace in my life?" Jesus says, you need to keep the law. You need to love God with all that you are and your neighbor as yourself. Then, the student takes it one step further and says, "Who is my neighbor?" Have you ever noticed that when God speaks to us, God tells us to reach out to grace? Embrace it. Hold on to it. Take all that you can. You can never take it all. And when we speak to God, we ask what is the least that we have to do in order to be involved. So the man says, "Who is my neighbor?"

So then Jesus tells that wonderful story about the good Samaritan. Here is a person who had every reason to say, "It is not my problem. That Jew has gotten himself into trouble. They don't even think we Samaritans are humans. It is not my problem." But he didn't. He brought hope to hopelessness – and in that bringing of hope to the hopeless, he brought the very face of grace into that person's life. Paul brings it full circle in Galatians when he calls us to bear each other's burdens and so fulfill the law of Christ. You can't walk away from it. What began as an echo in Genesis is a shout in Galatians. Who is responsible here? We are. We are to bear one another's burdens.

Of course, we can answer the question any way we choose. We can walk away from the problem and pretend it doesn't exist. But the Lord says we are responsible.

I am so proud of you. Everywhere I go, everyone I meet, I tell them I am so proud to be a part of what I consider to be one of the great congregations in this nation. When you could have left, you chose to stay. Not to just survive and hang on but to thrive and to do everything you could to minister to this community and to this whole city. But it is not enough. We are to take the little bit that we have and give it to the Lord, and he does the impossible with it. This is what God wants to do in your life and in our life as a congregation. Taking hope and grace to those in need. We will stay here, where the need is, because we are responsible.

The Vocation of
the Christian Father

Deuteronomy 6:5–8

This sermon is clearly thematic or topical rather than ex-pository. It was first preached in 1995 as a Father's Day sermon — an occasion which, like Mother's Day, presents the preacher with significant pastoral/homiletical chal-lenges, some of which are alluded to in the introduction. The structure of the message follows a systematic moral rather than textual logic. It is full of concrete, rule-type exhortations. It also involves a significant number of data citations, more than usual for a sermon but, as we have indicated, sometimes necessary in ethically ori-ented preaching. It is a sermon that steps on toes in classic prophetic style. — dpg

It's Father's Day. You may be expecting a Father's Day sermon. Well, that's okay, because that's what you're going to get. But not without some hesitation on my part.

Like many other preachers, I hesitate to preach a Father's Day message because of the pain that Father's Day and the whole issue of fatherhood mean for many people. I don't know this congregation, but I do know that if you are at all representative of our culture, some of you had pretty bad experiences with your father. So as you look back it hurts to remember. Others of you may be men who want to be fathers but have not yet had that opportunity and may never have it. I think here of the pain of the involuntarily childless couple. I think also of single men who want to be married and have children.

For those of you in these situations, God speaks a word of comfort today. If your father was not what he should have been, remember that God is the perfect heavenly Father and that even now he is here for you. For those who would like to but do not have children, remember that God the Father comforts the afflicted and the sorrowful. He wants to comfort you even now.

Having said this, it still seems important on this day to consider the task of the Christian father. This is an issue that God the Father cares very deeply about, for he has revealed through his Word much about this subject. And it is an issue that matters very deeply in our own culture at this time – a culture that is experiencing a crisis in the family and especially in fatherhood.

Today I want to offer a sermon on the vocation of the Christian father. It comes from the Word of God. It is also deeply affected by my own experiences – both as the son of a wonderful father and as the father of three young children myself.

I want to make four points. First, the vocation or calling of the Christian father begins with *being present* for his children. Second, a father must *do no harm* to his children. Third, a father must *do good* for his children in some specific ways that the Bible lays out. Finally, fathers should take time to *celebrate* and enjoy the precious gifts God has given them.

1. Be There

The Bible talks a lot about the responsibilities of fathers, but it doesn't say much about the first prerequisite for fulfilling these responsibilities: simply being there. Excepting death, a father's presence is assumed in the Bible. But in our time – a time of "father absence" and "father hunger," as some writers put it – we must reemphasize the importance of a father's presence in the life of his children.

Being there has to do first with the problem of out-of-wedlock births. Approximately 30 percent of American children today are born into homes in which the father is absent from the very beginning. This is up from 5 percent in

1960. This is an extraordinary figure with equally extraordinary consequences. Three out of ten children in this country never know or relate to their father.

The issue of being there also involves our nation's divorce epidemic. There were 1.2 million divorces in the United States in 1991, three times as many as in 1960. Each year divorce affects over one million children, leaving them in single-parent homes; 90 percent of children in single-parent homes live with their mothers. Fewer than 60 percent of today's American children live in a home with both of their biological parents.

Men, the first and basic requirement for positively influencing your children is a solid marriage. As Paul says in Ephesians, "Love your wives, just as Christ loved the church" (Ephesians 5:25). Care for your marriage. This does not mean that you can't be present in your child's life if you are divorced. Absolutely not. If this is your situation, it is extremely important to be present to your children the best way you can. But for all who are not divorced, the Word of God is clear. Nurture your marriage for the sake of your children and spouse as well as to obey God.

Two other issues are related to being there. One is your *physical* availability to your children. Most men wrestle with the issue of how to relate work and family. Some of you work in jobs that take you away from home quite frequently, either on out-of-town trips or simply long hours where you are. A lot of times nothing can be done about this. But look closely at your situation every now and again. From experience I can testify that sometimes overwork creeps up on us, and our families get neglected without our really knowing it. We need to make use of whatever opportunities we have to keep that under control and to spend time with our families. It may even involve a job change. But family comes before work.

The other issue here has to do with a father's *emotional* presence. Some men are "present in the body but absent in the spirit" when they are with their children. They either have no energy for the responsibilities of parenting (perhaps drained by their eighty-hour-a-week job), no knowledge of these responsibilities, or no commitment to undertaking them, perhaps thinking that their contribution to the family consists solely of bringing home a good paycheck.

Men, children are hurt by your emotional absence. Have you become the kind of father whose family time consists of watching television and falling asleep on the couch? Be present to your children. Be involved.

2. Do No Harm

Next we turn to the painful matter of fathers who are indeed present in their children's lives but in destructive, harmful, and abusive ways. After the issue of presence, the next question for a Christian father is whether or not he is doing harm to his children.

Tragically, fathers harm their children in a variety of ways. One must name sexual abuse as a fundamental offense and one that is absolutely forbidden in the Scriptures (Leviticus 18:6). God commanded the death penalty for sexual abuse in the Old Testament. One can hardly imagine a more fundamental assault on a child's well-being.

Other forms of physical abuse that are also devastating and all too common are punching, slapping, beating, and worse. Here the issue of corporal punishment, like spanking, is raised. While the Bible does at times indicate the usefulness of this form of discipline, physical punishment can easily cross an invisible but real line between discipline and abuse. Often this happens when a father is frustrated about other things and takes it out on his kids. Fathers, be alert for this and please get help if you find yourself harming your children.

Verbal or emotional abuse can also devastate a child. Statements or other forms of behavior that denigrate a child's worth, intelligence, physical appearance, potential, or lovableness are not forgotten. They can hurt as much as any beating. Even one such incident can scar a child; a consistent pattern of such behavior constitutes verbal or emotional abuse.

Fathers can also be a source of harm to their children through a variety of other serious character flaws. For example, men struggling with substance abuse problems or committing criminal activities bring danger into children's lives. One is re-minded of the teaching of Jesus: "Every good tree bears good fruit, but a bad tree bears bad fruit. A good tree cannot bear bad fruit, and a bad tree cannot bear good fruit" (Matthew 7:17–18). Children need fathers who are "good trees" rather than bad ones. They cannot afford to be fathered by the morally decaying man whose character is like a rotting tree. A child who tries to hang on to such a father discovers the branch snapping off in her hands, leaving her falling helplessly to the ground.

Don't be a dangerous father. That is exactly the opposite of what you are called to be.

3. Do Good

If you're there in your children's life, and if you are not doing any real harm, that's a start. If you are earning a decent living and providing for them, that is also important. But still, it is only a start. For the Word of God has much more in mind for Christian fathers.

First, fathers are called to offer spiritual instruction to their children. The importance of spiritual instruction of children is powerfully illustrated in our text from the book of Deuteron-omy. The commandments are to be "upon your hearts." This is a way of saying that loving God and doing his will are to be a father's most heartfelt concerns. Perhaps the first moral issue facing Christian fathers at this level is whether they are, in fact, committed Christians. Are you?

These commandments are to be "impress[ed] on your chil-dren." This is supposed to happen through regular spiritual instruction and nurture at home. You can't leave all the "Chris-tianity" to the church. It has to happen at home! Men, did you know that many women report that their Christian husbands are uninterested in, if not hostile to, the idea of family worship and Bible study at home? That's so wrong, because the Bible clearly teaches that men must be deeply involved at home in instructing their children in the way of faith.

How do you do this? Through daily devotionals and Bible reading at dinnertime, morning prayers before school, evening prayers at bedtime, and other approaches. It also means being prayerfully alert to the opportunity to offer spiritual instruction at other times, as your children "walk along the road" of life.

Fathers are also called to offer moral instruction to their children.

> My son, pay attention to what I say;
>   listen closely to my words.
> Do not let them out of your sight,
>   keep them within your heart;
> for they are life to those who find them
>   and health to a man's whole body.
>   (Proverbs 4:20–22)

Many fathers today have lost an awareness of their critical role in the moral instruction of their children. But the Bible clearly teaches that fathers have significant responsibilities in this area. How our children need our help in learning how they should live!

The apostle Paul indicated this indirectly but clearly in the following statement about his own ministry: "We dealt with each of you as a father deals with his own children, encouraging, comforting and urging you to live lives worthy of God" (1 Thessalonians 2:11–12). Teach them about character, about what kind of people they should be. Teach them about conduct – the rules for living that God lays out in his holy Word. Show them how to live; they need you.

4. Celebrate

I want to close by inviting you to a level of fathering that goes beyond all that I have said thus far, even though what I have said is pretty demanding in and of itself. It has to do with celebrating your children for the sacred gifts from God that they are.

Celebrate your children by building a close personal relationship with each of them. Seek opportunities to spend one-on-one time with each child. Befriend them, nurture them, love them. Each of them.

Celebrate your children by creatively looking for interesting new ways to play with and enjoy them. Try not to leave all your energy and creativity at work. Save some for your children, and make family time a delight.

Celebrate your children by enjoying transcendent and joyful moments with them. Have you ever had a moment like this? Perhaps it is at bedtime or on the playground or while taking a walk. In a moment of time, you experience a wave of recognition of the extraordinary worth and preciousness of your child. You feel a wave of gratitude and profound joy. You worship God as you celebrate your child.

Such moments can happen only if a father is present with his children. They require that a father do no harm to his children. They are rooted in a father's doing good for his children, in the daily provision of both material and spiritual goods. They are made possible by a father's involvement, commitment, passion, and love for his little ones.

Moments like this help us catch a glimpse of God's reasons for bringing new life into the world – and for entrusting new life to frail and fallible human beings like ourselves. In our joy, we see a reflection of God's joy.

Men, may you not only fulfill your basic responsibilities as fathers, but also taste the joy of God through your children.

A Moment to Savor/
A Lifetime to Regret

2 Samuel 13:1–22

We've decided at Walnut Street to use a thematic approach to Sunday morning worship. Our themes run for the full year with emerging subplots developing within each theme. In 1995 our worship theme was simply "Strong Ties." Each month offered an unfolding of that basic theme. In May the theme unfolded as "Strong Ties to a Working Model of Faith – the Family." On May 7 we explored human sexuality using 2 Samuel 13:1–22, the story of Amnon's rape of his half-sister, Tamar. This sermon offers a thematic treatment of Christian sexual morality based on an important but neglected Old Testament narrative. – rhl

My wife and I had a lot of household wedding showers prior to our wedding. I suppose everybody has stories they share about such showers. Nearly every couple receives a gift they can't identify and don't have a clue about. They don't even know if they ought to put it on display or what room it should be displayed in. We had our share of those gifts. But our best story probably would be the seventeen blankets we received. They might have come in handy if we hadn't moved to the subtropical climate of New Orleans within a year of our wedding day. We didn't even need one blanket there. Have you ever tried to store seventeen blankets in a two-bedroom apartment with only three closets? That is all the closets we had, and one of those was a coat closet. We ended up using blankets for couch pillows. Anyone who came to visit us received a free blanket. The mailman got a blanket at Christmas time. The guy who tried to steal the grill off our deck got a blanket. It took a long time to get rid of seventeen blankets in New Orleans.

But by far, the best gift we received did not come from human hands. It didn't even come in that wedding time frame. It was a gift God gave us when God created us – the gift of the ability to express love and fear and all of the great intangibles of life sexually. It is God's wedding gift. And like so many things from the hand of God in the world today, it is tragically abused.

Last fall, when we were praying and pondering over what God would want us to consider throughout this year, it seemed that through the month of May and beyond we ought to look at the strong ties God's grace gives to us and offer a working model of family life. You have heard a lot of sermons about how to have a Christian home, and bookstore shelves are cluttered with books on the topic, but until many of us reconnect with God through forgiveness of the mistakes, miscues, and sin we have created in our lives because of the poor choices we've made sexually, all that other talk about homes won't matter much.

I have permission to tell you this story. It's about a friend of mine, a dear friend. He and his wife have two daughters. When I last saw the youngest of those two daughters – let's call her Jo – she was in middle school. My friend and his wife are hardworking, successful, middle-class people. When they moved because of his work, they decided the public school system in the city they were moving to was not what they wanted for their daughters. And so, at great expense, they enrolled their two daughters in a fairly exclusive private school. I'm telling you these details, not to brag about him, but to let you know that these two parents not only gave time to their children, but they did the best they could to bless their children.

When Jo, the youngest of these two daughters, was about a junior, she met a young boy who also attended that exclusive school. They began to date, and soon the dating took on a rather serious mode and they went steady. They decided that they loved each other. Jo had been brought up in a Christian home, and her values were deeply embedded in her life. But one November night, after the couple had had a few beers, they exchanged intimacy for intercourse. There is a big difference between the two. A couple of nights later, they were together again. The young man assumed that again they would exchange intimacy for intercourse. But the guilt was greater than the young woman could bear, and she said no. It wasn't very long before this love that was a budding romance was a withered love. He had other places to go and other people to see.

A few weeks later, another boy, also in this exclusive school, asked Jo out, and they agreed to go on a date. Early in the evening he made advances on her sexually. She simply said that she was not that kind of person. His words to her broke her. He looked at her and said, "That is not what your former boyfriend said about you."

As a result, Jo decided she couldn't face her classmates. She has been through three schools since then. And her own father, who loves her dearly, told me last week, "I don't know what I am going to do. The crowd she's running with now – well, they are just sorry. And I see more and more evidence every day that she is taking on the characteristics of the crowd she is running with."

We can pretend all we want to that we have all kinds of moral values and that we are morally upright people, but there are moments we savor that yield lifetimes of regret. If nothing else, the passage of Scripture read in your hearing this morning should remind us that all sexual misconduct is sin. We can cast it in a different light. We can talk about our First Amendment right of freedom of expression, our right to do what we want because we are adults, and how certain sexual activities are victimless, but sexual misconduct is still sin.

I heard those sermons when I was a child and when I was a teenager. I heard them from embarrassed preachers who didn't really want to talk on the subject and who would not talk about it in a frank and honest way. I find myself doing some of the same things. They would always say to me that sex outside of marriage is wrong, and all I ever wanted was for someone to tell me why. I mean, my mother told me it was wrong. My dad told me that it was sin. But nobody ever told me why. Maybe it was because they didn't think about it enough. I don't know. But I now know why sexual misconduct is sin. It's sin because it takes a human being and it makes of them an object. If that young girl could get past her mortification, she would stand here today and say to us, "I was used. I was an object. No one who loves you genuinely would do what that young man did with my reputation, my feelings."

I am not here to say that all sexual misconduct is perpetrated by men against women. We are equal opportunity abusers in these relationships. But you and I need to understand that God has given human beings a very precious gift – the gift of intimacy – to be ultimately expressed in marriage. And what happens too often is that we step outside of those boundaries and in a form of misconduct abuse the gifts. Those moments are filled with regret.

When I counsel young couples, I draw them a pyramid on a piece of paper. I draw a line through the bottom inch or so of it and say that this represents one level of communication, the level we engage in most often during the day. "Hi. How are you? How are you doing? Isn't the weather wonderful? Man, isn't it hot?" I don't give much of myself in that kind of communication. If someone were to walk away from me after such a conversation and say, "What a jerk!" I would look at that person and say, "You don't know me. You don't know what kind of a jerk I really can be." I don't give much of myself in that kind of communication, so I don't risk very much.

But above that level, there is another level. Casual friends know me better. I give more of myself in that kind of communication. I risk more. And above that level is another level – very close friends. They know me extremely well. I really risk myself at that level. If they say I'm a jerk, it is because they know all my quirks. And still above that level is a level of family members who have known me all of my life and therefore know me very, very well. But above that is the little corner, the little crown, of that pyramid, and that is reserved for Judy. She knows me best of all. When she says I am a jerk, she knows what she is talking about. She can quote you chapter and verse on my jerkhood. I risk everything with her, and our sexuality is an expression of our communication with each other. Nothing is held back. That is how it is intended to be. That is why sexual misconduct is a sin; it abuses the most precious form of communication human beings have. It treats the other person as an object, and that is wrong. Such abuse goes on in our world too much of the time.

Tamar and Amnon are great examples. Here is a crown prince of Israel, the man potentially in line for the throne, and he abuses the most precious gift he has and his half-sister has. Victimless? Let's be honest enough to say no. There are always victims.

The second thing we learn as we study this passage of Scripture is that not only is sexual misconduct a sin because it violates that intimacy and it demeans and treats human beings as objects, but there is another problem here. After the intercourse has occurred, there is no intimacy. Tamar misunderstood what was happening. She thought that Amnon wanted to marry her. That society, the society of David, was almost as sexually confused and chaotic as ours. Nevertheless, what was happening in the bedroom of the crown prince was wrong.

Thinking that Amnon wants to marry her, Tamar tells him to wait and that David will not withhold from him what he desires. He will let them marry. But Amnon rapes her. Did you see what the Bible says next? It says that his hatred was far greater than his love for her was before, and he decides that he wants nothing to do with her. He refuses to accept responsibility for his own actions. She says, and she is right, that what he does next is even more wrong, if that is possible, than what he did at first.

A lot of people in our world today say that there is nothing wrong with sexual activity between consenting adults, that it is victimless. But that is not true; there are all kinds of victims. The Bible says here that the young woman leaves as a totally different person than when she came into that room. She went into the room a princess, she leaves a desolate woman. She went into the room a child of the king. She leaves still a child of the king but no longer does she feel that it is a privilege to be in a royal household. Now she will live in disgrace. Victimless? The young man is also going to be a victim. His half-brother's hatred for him is intense, and ultimately his half brother will conspire to have him killed. Victimless? Even the king is enraged. But the problem with King David's rage is that he can do nothing about it. Why? Because there is enough sin in his own life in the same areas that he really has no room to say anything whatsoever. If you hear a sad, strange echo in this passage of Scripture from an earlier passage, you will begin to understand that this sounds a whole lot like what David himself had already done with Bathsheba. Victimless? No. There are all kinds of victims in this story as there are all kinds of victims in this room. You and I need to understand that part of the victimization that takes place here is when we refuse to accept responsibility for who we are, for what we do with life.

I have just finished reading a biography on the life of John F. Kennedy written by Thomas Reeves entitled *A Question of Character* (Rockland, Calif.: Prima Publishing, 1992, 415). I enjoyed this biography immensely. In the last few pages of his book, Reeves says that a president, while he or she may have great abilities, tremendous intellectual capacity and political skill, and all kinds of advisors upon whom he can draw for information, still must ultimately take all the information that he or she might have and finally make a decision. At that point, character matters, for decisions emerge out of that character. What is true of a chief executive is true of everyone else as well. Character matters. It does make a difference who we are and how we look at life. You can decide before you put yourself at risk what your answers will be. Before you ever involve yourself sexually, you can make the decision that you will guard your heart and avoid that pain. Character matters. It matters in your life. It matters in all of our lives.

There is one last thing I want us to recognize out of this passage of Scripture, and that is the ripple effect. I have already told you that there are all kinds of victims in this passage of Scripture. But do you know that the course of an entire nation may have been changed? This young man is the crown prince. He will die. His murderer will eventually die. And the throne will become Solomon's. David is going to die a little bit inside because of this. Tamar will never be the same. Israel will never have the same respect she could have had for her royal family and household. Oh, there are victims aplenty.

What I want you to understand is that, yes, God's grace can heal. If you have been a victim, God's grace can be sufficient for you. But what I want you to hear first of all is that God's grace can also be sufficient for you before you become a victim. The world needs quiet examples of men and women who graciously exchange their intimacy with each other only in marriage. Will you make that your commitment this day?

The Code of a Man of Honor

Job 31

This sermon was my first sermon (November 1996) to the students and community of Union University, a Southern Baptist school in Jackson, Tennessee. In terms of methodology, this sermon is an expository treatment of a fairly lengthy block of Scripture. The text surprises the hearer in the depth of its moral insight and in its contribution to a richer understanding of a fascinating biblical personage. This sermon essentially allows Job's "code of honor" to speak for itself, implicitly inviting hearers to draw their own comparative applications. The sermon is targeted for Christians attending Union, and it focuses on individual application. Interestingly enough, the social relevance of the sermon three years later may be even greater than when it was first preached. —dpg

Introduction: The Contemporary Quest for People of Honor

Do these names ring a bell? Jim and Tammy Faye Bakker, Jimmy Swaggart, Ivan Boesky, Michael Milken, Wade Boggs, Michael Irvin, Michael Jackson, Madonna, Gary Hart, Dick Morris.

On the one hand, this is a diverse list, representing the worlds of religion, business, sports, entertainment, and politics. On the other hand, the people on this list share one

118

thing in common – scandal. These are people who once were honored, but now by their dishonorable conduct, have lost that honor.

We live in a time in which honorable men and women are harder and harder to find. We are no longer surprised when we open the newspapers to discover that scandal has hit a local church, business, or university, not to mention the national level. Our naivete is gone. We know that just because someone holds a high position doesn't mean he or she can be trusted. As our expectations of our leaders decline, our cynicism about them increases.

Yet we – the world as well as the church – cannot quite give up the hope that someone, somewhere, will be as trustworthy and honorable as he or she appears to be. We continue to seek people of honor. We are hungry for them.

Literary Context

My text this morning is Job 31. It speaks directly to our concern.

You will remember the plight of Job. He was, the Bible says, a blameless and upright man who feared God and shunned evil (Job 1:1). At the beginning of the book, he is blessed with every good gift: family, health, home, property, happiness. His blameless life has captured the attention of God, who makes note of Job to Satan (uh, oh), who in turn asks for the opportunity to test Job and proceeds to destroy every single aspect of Job's happy life. Job's wife is spared, but she tells him to curse God and die, so she's not much help.

Job first responds to his calamity with seven days of silent grief, but then, increasingly, with the question Why? And especially, Why me? It is a question all too familiar to those of us who have watched the innocent suffer on this earth. It is a question some of us in this room have asked.

Job has three friends who come to help him. They're at their best when they sit silently with him that first week. But when they attempt to answer his question, they come back again and again to the same theme: Innocent people do not suffer calamity, and the guilty do not go unpunished. You have suffered calamity, therefore, you must be guilty of some major sin against God. Yet Job will not confess what he has not done. Tensions run high with his friends after about thirty chapters of this. I don't see them going out for pizza and a movie after this little conversation.

The text we are looking at today is part of Job's final word of defense. In chapter 29 he recalls with wistful sorrow the wonderful life he once enjoyed. In chapter 30 he grieves over all the calamity that has befallen him. And in chapter 31, our text, he mounts a final defense of his conduct against the charges of his so-called friends.

Job's Code of Honor

I am calling this text "Job's Code of Honor." One commentator says that it "reveals in exquisite terms the highest moral conscience in the Old Testament." It is a code of honor any of us would do well to study. And so we shall this morning.

The form Job's code takes is interesting. It is what is called "a negative confession." He lists about sixteen sins that, if he committed them, would have justly brought down upon his head all the suffering that he now experiences. Thus, we have the form, "If I have done so and so, then, yes, I deserve to lose my family and have the worst skin of any major patriarch in the region. But I have not done so and so, so my suffering is undeserved."

Let's look briefly at the sixteen particular sins that Job disavows. Turn them right-side-up, and we see a powerful code of honorable living. Try it out on your own life as we walk through it.

1. *Verse 5: "If I have walked in falsehood or...hurried after deceit...."* Job begins not with specific sins but with a general repudiation of an immoral way of life. Notice the implicit imagery of a journey – the moral life is a journey, a path one walks. The person of honor walks straight and true, keeps his feet on the path of right conduct and does not swerve from it. He is well aware of the ways in which one's foot can slip. To walk in falsehood or hurry after deceit is to allow a gap to

grow between public self-representation and the secret life of a secret self. It is to live a lie.

2. *Verse 7: "If my steps have turned from the path, if my heart has been led by my eyes, or if my hands have been defiled...."* Living a lie has its price. No longer is the heart governed by one's conscience and principles, but as here, by one's eyes and what happens to please or entice them. No longer are one's hands clean, but they are instead stained by the sins they have committed – a stain no soap can wash away. You have slipped off the path of honor and are at risk of tumbling down the hill to destruction.

3. *Verse 9: "If my heart has been enticed by a woman, or if I have lurked at my neighbor's door...."* Notice also verse 1, in which Job says that he "made a covenant with [his] eyes, not to look lustfully at a girl." Here Job takes on the issue of sexual sin, and with these three negative confessions, he has identified all three major aspects of such sin, which build upon each other: first, the lustful glance, gaze, or look; then, the transition from attracted eyes to an enticed heart, from a passing sensation to a growing intention; and finally, the lurking at the neighbor's door, meaning the definite intention now acted upon to violate the sanctity of another's marriage. Job's code rules out the lustful glance and thus cuts off other sins before they can take hold. Most of the people I mentioned at the beginning of this sermon were brought down by sexual sin. Job's words are indeed to be taken to heart.

4. *Verses 13–15: "If I have denied justice to my menservants and maidservants...."* A man or woman of honor treats all people as equals regardless of social rank or status. What a marvelous statement of what used to be called the fatherhood of God and the brotherhood of man. Job denies that he has ever abused his power to deny the rights of the men and women who served him and his family. He has listened to their grievances with respect in recognition of their human dignity, which matches his because of their common origin. How profoundly this passage speaks to issues of race and social class in our day.

5. *Verse 16: "If I have denied the desires of the poor or let the eyes of the widow grow weary...."* Every strand of

the biblical witness demands of people of faith a stance of generosity to the poor and special concern for the most vulnerable. Law, History, Wisdom, Prophets, Gospels, Epistles – all do. Job here denies any violation of this mandate. He has met not only the needs but also the desires of the poor. The eyes of the widow are weary from crying according to most commentators; Job has not looked hard-heartedly upon such misery but has instead acted to help. Would that we were as compassionate.

6. *Verses 17–18: "If I have kept my bread to myself...."* Here we catch a further glimpse of the depth and breadth of Job's generosity. He has not only shared his food with the orphan but has in fact taken him into his own home and raised him as a father; the same kind of care has been extended to the widow.

7. *Verses 19–20: "If I have seen anyone perishing for lack of clothing...."* Likewise, Job has offered warm clothing and coverings to those who lack them. As the weather cools, as winter comes to Jackson, these words have a particular resonance. Notice that there is no evidence that Job has sought to examine why the needy have need or to discern who are the worthy as opposed to the unworthy poor. That is our temptation. Job has simply met needs.

8. *Verses 21–22: "If I have raised my hand against the fatherless...."* The key words here are "knowing that I had influence in the court." Job was a rich man before calamity struck. Then, as now, rich people had opportunity to twist the justice system in their favor. It was all too easy to defraud a worker of his pay or to abuse an orphan or widow; these people lacked power or anyone to defend their interests. It was one person's word against another's, and the one who had friends at the city gate or in the courtroom prevailed. But the Old Testament consistently demands that in such cases those with power were to defend the vulnerable, not exploit them. And so Job denies that he has ever violated this explicit command. His imagery about his just punishment here is quite striking, isn't it?

9. *Verse 24: "If I have put my trust in gold...."* At this point, Job is really getting into sensitive territory, which we

might like him to avoid. But there he is, warning us of the danger of turning money and property into idols before which we bow down and to which we give our very lives. Job denies that he has fallen prey to that subtle but oh so corrosive idolatry. In God, not gold, we trust.

10. *Verse 25: "If I have rejoiced over my great wealth...."* Indeed, Job has avoided even celebrating overmuch the wealth and property he has been given. He knows these are – were – good gifts. But they are not worthy of excessive delight or celebration. They are useful for all that can be done with them for others. They bring a measure of pleasure, but they do not lie at the center of what matters most in life. Only God can be found there.

Earlier I said that most of my opening names had been brought down by sexual sin. Most of the rest of them were brought down right here – in gold we trust and in rejoicing over great wealth and the intoxicating quest for more.

11. *Verses 26–28: "If I have regarded the sun...or the moon...."* Here at last we find Job denying any form of idol worship. This is the first and only vertical command that Job addresses in his code of honor, a fact that is striking in itself. He denies that he has been enticed by the glory of the sun and moon to any worship of them. The reference to kissing appears to reflect a Syrian practice of throwing kisses of worship to the sun and moon. Job has had none of it.

12. *Verses 29–30: "If I have rejoiced at my enemy's misfortune...."* I do not need to remind you that rejoicing at the downfall of one's enemies is a very common human feeling; and cursing one's enemies is a very common human behavior. But Job here reflects the highest of biblical teaching in denying that such behavior is consistent with his moral code. He will not rejoice in an enemy's downfall. What about us?

13. *Verses 31–32: "If the men of my household have never said...."* These verses point to Job's hospitality. The people in Job's household have been entertained lavishly, and he has also demonstrated hospitality to the stranger. Hospitality in that culture was understood to be a major moral obligation, and Job denies any violation of that obligation.

14. *Verses 33–34: "If I have concealed my sin as men*

do.... " Here Job makes an interesting point. Part of his code is confession of sin. He has not concealed his sin in an effort to appear perfect before his neighbors; instead, he has been willing to publicly admit where he erred. Contrast this with Adam, who hid from God after his sin. Our temptation since Adam is to descend into the falsehood and deceit that Job earlier disavowed by giving the appearance of infallibility. Job denies he has done this.

15. *Verse 38: "If my land cries out against me.... "* Earlier Job had been charged with abuse of his power as a large landowner; here he denies any such charge. If it were true, the land would cry out against him, as did the land that absorbed Abel's blood when he was murdered by his brother Cain. But he denies that he has abused that power and thus caused the land to proverbially weep.

16. *Verse 39: "If I have devoured its yield without payment.... "* Here Job refers explicitly to what he as a powerful landowner could have done. He could have hired tenant farmers to work the fields, received the fruit of their labor, and then not paid them. They would have had no recourse, and it would have broken the very spirit of the tenant farmers – maybe even killed them, as it reads in some other translations. But Job has not done this.

Application

And so Job finishes his defense. He has lived according to this moral code and is willing to defend himself before God on the basis of it. It is indeed a remarkable code of ethics and stands as one of the high points of the scriptural moral witness. Why is it so special?

First, it is a holistic code. It is remarkably comprehensive. It addresses both actions and attitudes. A healthy Christian moral life involves getting both our interior life right – our thoughts, motives, feelings, and attitudes – and our exterior life right. I fear that we tend to be so concerned with attitudes that we don't pay sufficient attention to actions.

Second, it addresses both the vertical and horizontal aspects of God's claim on our lives. By vertical I mean the human-God relationship. By horizontal I mean our moral obligations to others. Both are addressed throughout the Bible. But I fear that we tend to be so concerned with the vertical that we forget the horizontal.

Third, it addresses both personal and social moral obligations. Personal obligations include things like sexual behavior and attitudes toward money. Social obligations include areas such as treatment of the poor and the vulnerable and employees. Job mixes them freely. But I fear that we tend to emphasize the personal at the expense of the social.

Finally, it addresses what today might be considered both liberal and conservative moral concerns. Christian liberals tend to be concerned with hunger and homelessness and political injustice; conservatives tend to be concerned with sexual morality and truthfulness. Job is concerned about both. He would find our labels unhelpful to say the least. I fear we have trouble thinking beyond them.

Conclusion

If we read Job's code of honor in light of the New Testament and the example of Jesus Christ, we might be inclined to critique Job for his apparent belief that his life was so upright that he deserved God's blessing. We Christian types are inclined to emphasize that no one is righteous in God's sight. We are saved by God's grace, not Job's code.

This is certainly true. But let us not therefore dispense with Job's code of honor and other morally demanding biblical texts. God's grace does mean forgiveness of our sins. But it also means the availability of a new spiritual power that makes it possible for the moral quality of our lives not just to meet but to exceed the standards we find in Job's code of honor.

Let us not use God's grace as an excuse for moral laziness. Let us lay our lives against Job's code to see how we are doing.

A Proper Quest

Psalm 127

This 1996 sermon responds to the presidential race, which had made its appearance in Louisville in an extraordinary way over the previous several days. It also has as its background the rising toll of drug-related violence in the downtown area. Our "First Church" setting is an ideal platform for addressing the powers that be, but for precisely that reason the proper boundaries of such address must be guarded carefully. This sermon lays out some of the key theological and moral principles for local congregational political involvement and points ultimately to the centrality of our sovereign God in all of life. — rhl

Any way you want to slice it, this past week has been extraordinary for the city of Louisville. Five men have visited our city this week who are seeking the two highest elected positions in our nation. They have all come to our city and spoken about what they intend to do should we choose to spend our vote for their ticket this fall. Now, I'm sure that as children of God you will be responsible citizens and exercise your right to vote. But over the next seventy-one days you are going to have to sort through a maze of all kinds of rhetoric designed, first, to bolster a particular position and candidate and, second, to drive down the positive image that you feel toward their rivals for office. In seventy-one days you will have to cast your ballot.

Make no mistake about it. As we close out this century and move to the opening of yet another century – and another millennium – what you will be doing is nothing less than selecting the chief architects for society. That is really what we do with our electoral process. We elect a president who we want to have as the chief architect of our society. You will readily recognize that one party will say, "As architect I see a society in which we diminish the role of government so we can enhance the role of the citizen." At the same time, another contender for that same position of chief architect of society will say, "No, from my position and my party's platform, I see that there is a legitimate role for government and it helps to level out the peaks and valleys that we would otherwise have. It is important that you elect my party so that we will have a more just and fair society." There will be other positions in between those two. But the election is all about whose architectural vision for society you will accept.

There is yet another architect – the chief architect. He is not only the chief architect of this society but of all societies. His blueprint, his platform, for what he envisions for a society is found in Psalm 127. It is the song of ascent that I read to you a moment ago. You probably already know that there is a curious geographical quirk about Jerusalem. From all the region of Israel, one has to go *up* to Jerusalem. Annually the Jewish people made a pilgrimage up to Jerusalem to worship God. As they made their way into the city, they sang some of the beautiful psalms that are collected for us in this portion of the book of Psalms called the Songs of Ascent. Psalm 127 is a song and prayer of petition. In it you will discover a wonderful, grand design for society. Today we are talking about what this church will be in its future. Please hear two or three things from the outset that relate closely to the high-powered visitors we've had here this week.

First, this church is not a political instrument. We have no party affiliation as a church. The reason we have no party affiliation as a church is because God has no party affiliation. We will not endorse candidates from this pulpit. The only candidate we ever intend to endorse from this pulpit is Jesus Christ. Having said that, I must say to you that we have a valuable mission and a role to fill in this city. But we must understand what our role is if we are going to be able to plug ourselves into the life of one of the great communities in America. This is a wonderful place to live, a grand place to rear one's family. But it can be better

and it must be better. It will become better when we stop looking to human instruments as architects of this community and
go back to acknowledging God as the only chief architect. If
we would understand that God has crafted a plan for this and
every society, and if we would get into our hearts the desire to
promote no other plan except our Savior's, then we would be
doing the greatest service possible for our community.

We live in an era when two words have become extraordi-
narily important to this culture. We use them with frequency:
diversity and *pluralism*. There are great things to be said about
a diverse community, a pluralistic society. There is nothing
wrong with those words. I well remember being interviewed
by a reporter from the *Courier-Journal* when I accepted the
invitation you gave me to come and be your pastor. I was asked
why I would want to come to this church. Part of my reason
then is still a part of my reason today for thanking God for the
privilege of serving this church. I believe that here in the heart
of this city is a very diverse congregation, and its diversity is its
richness. The fact that we do not all look alike or sound alike or
come from the same zip code, the fact that we have different
opinions about a whole range of issues, is not something that
we should be ashamed of. It is part of the very rich fabric that is
woven together to make this congregation. It is a plus, folks, to
be diverse. I'm glad and grateful to God that my children grow
up in a community of faith where not all of us look alike, sound
alike, and act alike. We are bound here in this place – coming
from all different points of view – by a common love for the
Lord Jesus Christ. I like that.

But I must say to you that every position in life has its down
side, and the down side of our diversity is that sometimes we
have decided that we should set God out on the edge of our
community life because we haven't wanted to offend someone.
But the reason we exist is to promote the position that the chief
architect of society, God our heavenly Father, has presented to
us in Christ Jesus. There is no plurality, there is no diversity
so significant and so important that we should ever abandon
that position. If we ever abandon that, we have nothing else to
proclaim. Then the doors of this great old church might just as
well be closed.

Having said that, I feel it's time for us to stop assuming that someone else will point out that God has an architectural design for our society. That is our responsibility, to present that plan to our community without reservation, without qualification. It is a good plan. The Bible says that God as chief architect builds societies. He builds them one home at a time, one family at a time. Guess what, folks? In the next seventy-one days you are going to hear about the family from every point of view on the political spectrum. Everyone is going to claim that he or she is the advocate for, and the candidate of, family values. But I want to tell you something: Before anybody ever heard that phrase and thought it fit into a political campaign, God was the author of family values. Our God builds societies one family at a time, one family unit stacked on another.

Three different places in the first two verses of this simple little song say that when God is ignored or left out of the basic building blocks of society, there is a gaping, empty hole. The English word that translates the Hebrew of this text says it is a vanity. It is empty. That word can't begin to fully describe what we are discussing when we talk about the emptiness that godlessness in the families of our community has created. The Bible says that when God is left out of the building of homes, there is this awful, empty, gaping chasm. When God is left out of the building of a city, you can't come up with anything else to fill the gap or say that there is meaning and purpose here. A society that looks at God as though God should be shoved to the corner is a society that will soon lose its purpose. This church needs to be one of the places from which this city hears that there is a necessity for us to embrace God, because otherwise there is no purpose in our existence.

The second thing we discover in this passage is that nothing fills that chasm other than God. Listen to that second verse once again. "In vain you rise early and stay up late, toiling for food to eat – for he grants sleep to those he loves." Our divine candidate's platform says that it is important to understand that God has given you work to do with your hands. Every now and then someone will come up to me and ask what it is like to work in church. Isn't it a little strange to work in church? And children will ask, "What is it like to work for God?" I am the only person they know who does that, because they look around and Mom and Dad are doing other things. Well, I work in church – that is true. But until you see what *you* do as a mission and a work from God, you will never have the kind of satisfaction you ought to have. God has called all of you to be ministers. Where he has planted you, you are a minister.

Some people are spending their lives toiling in their work yet are as empty as can be. Why? Because they have ignored God. It is a terrible price to pay. I have stood beside a lot of senior adults in my lifetime and listened to them as they talked to me about the end of their lives. I have never yet heard one say, "I wish I had worked a few more hours." I have never yet heard anybody say, "I wish I had earned a few more dollars." But I have heard a lot of them say, "I wish I had served God more faithfully and consistently." And I have heard a lot of them say, "I wish I had spent more time with my children." Nothing – not what you do with your hands, not the money you have, not the influence you wield over other people – nothing you will ever have will bridge that chasm. Nothing except Christ.

I also want you to see from this beautiful psalm that our society is perpetuated in our children. We cannot afford to have a society where children are viewed as a disposal commodity. It is time for us to say that our society as crafted by the chief architect is a society in which children are viewed for what they really are – wonderful, precious gifts from God. And until every child has the opportunity to live in an environment where he or she is safe and well and whole and is given opportunities to discover who God is and what God can do in his or her life, our work is not done.

Nor has the gospel touched every life as it should. That's what we will be about. From the heart of this city, God is calling you and me to a mission. He is calling us to a mission of helping to build this community one home at a time, home upon home. God is calling us to recognize that each one of us is a minister. We minister through what we do. From the heart of this city, God is saying that every generation needs to be renewed in Christ. That's the message this church will be proclaiming. That is why we choose to stay here in downtown Louisville, and that is what I call each of us to recommit to this morning.

Ambition

Matthew 20:20–28

This 1995 sermon was offered not to a local congregation but to a chapel audience at Southern Baptist Theological Seminary where I was teaching at the time. Like many morally focused sermons, it is addressed at least as much to the preacher as to the congregation. The sermon is instructive in its effort to identify and address with appropriate nuances a morally significant character concern. The audience of ministers and ministers-to-be also affects the approach taken. —dpg

Introduction

In the February 6, 1995, issue of *Newsweek*, religion writer Kenneth Woodward wrote a provocative little article called, "Whatever Happened to Sin?" In it he made this observation about the preaching that goes on in our churches:

> Many clergy, who are competing in a buyer's market, feel they cannot afford to alienate. To be sure, liberal ministers condemn such "systemic" social evils as racism and sexism. . . . But their voices are strangely muffled on subjects close to home – like divorce, pride, greed, and overweening personal ambition. Fundamentalist preachers still excoriate abortion, pornography, and other excesses of an anything-goes society. But these jeremiads are fists shaken at the world outside, not fingers pointed at those in the pews.

I don't want to be the kind of Christian preacher or teacher whose voice is "strangely muffled on a subject close to home," the kind who all the time "shakes his fist at the world outside" the walls of the church while ignoring the problems within. Woodward is right – we do have more than enough of that kind of preaching available. Therefore, I would like to take up the good columnist's challenge. From his list of topics, I pick ambition, one of those moral issues that affects all of us but that we never seem to talk about. And, as Woodward suggests, my concern is not with other people's ambition out there in the world, but with our own ambition here in the church. So let's explore the place of ambition in the Christian life, especially in the life of the Christian minister.

1. What Is Ambition?

What is ambition?

Mother Zebedee and her sons came to Jesus one day. They had a small matter to discuss with him. Just one little favor to ask. Not wanting the other ten disciples (and *their* mothers) to overhear, they pulled Jesus aside for a private little huddle.

I wonder if Jesus had to suppress a smile when he responded, "What is it you want?"

Mrs. Zebedee, speaking for her sons, fell to her knees. "Grant that one of these two sons of mine may sit at your right and the other at your left in the kingdom."

Ambition. James, John, and their mother had it. The Republicans who are running for president, already making weekly trips to snowy New Hampshire – they have it. The man who currently sits in the White House has it. Ambition.

What about us? Do we – Southern Seminary students, staff, administrators, faculty, guests – do we have ambition? If we do, is that good or bad? Or both? Or neither? Ambition is a slippery word. We need greater clarity about its meaning. Let's define ambition as *an earnest desire for some type of achievement or status.*

Sometimes when we use the word *ambition*, we are focusing on the "earnest desire" part of its meaning. If we describe a person as "ambitious," we are simply saying that he or she has an awful lot of that "earnest desire" to do or be something.

Other times we use the word *ambition* to refer to the

achievement or status sought – the goal toward which that "earnest desire" is directed. Thus, we might say of someone that "it has been her lifelong ambition to be famous."

The word *ambition* is not found in our text this morning. However, ambition itself certainly is, in both aspects of its meaning.

We see an awful lot of ambition here. What audacity Mrs. Zebedee and her sons had to approach Jesus with a request like this! How long do you think they had been planning and preparing for this moment? Do you think the three of them debated what might be the best strategy for asking Jesus this question? "Should *we all* approach him, or just mother? What time of day might be best? Should we try to get him alone? Hey, wait a minute, I've got it. Why don't we get Uncle Zach to create a diversion while we corner Jesus and pop the question?"

And we also see the particular object of their ambition. As Jesus headed toward Jerusalem for that decisive Passover week, James and John wanted to position themselves as the top two disciples in the group of twelve. They wanted to be Jesus' "right-hand" and "left-hand" men when he came into his kingdom. Of course, they completely misunderstood what Jesus' kingdom was about. Nevertheless, they wanted leadership in it. And Mother wanted that for them; she wanted it very badly indeed.

2. A Moral Evaluation of Ambition

But the ambition of James, John, and their mother didn't get a very good response that day. This leads us to an evaluation of the morality of ambition.

In the history of the church, ambition has often received a negative response. Consider a representative quotation, from Bernard of Clairvaux, a twelfth-century mystic: "Ambition is a secret poison, the father of [spite] and mother of hypocrisy, the moth of holiness and cause of madness, crucifying and disquieting all that it takes hold of." So tell us, Bernard, what do you really think of ambition?

The condemnation of ambition is common outside the

church as well. For example, the Tao te Ching reads, "There is no guilt greater than to approve ambition."

But the verdict on ambition is not unanimous either inside or outside the church. Lord Charnwood, a biographer of Abraham Lincoln, wrote, "Ambition . . . should be frankly recognized as a part of Christian duty." Mark Twain advised, "Keep away from people who try to belittle your ambitions. Small people always do that, but the really great make you feel that you, too, can become great." J. H. Oldham wrote, "Christianity . . . recognizes that ambition is of the essence of religion."

Well, which is it? Is ambition of God or of the devil?

To answer, let's once more break ambition down into the two parts of its meaning. Let's think first about that "earnest desire" to accomplish or be something.

This "desire" is a mysterious thing. Most people who have a fair amount of that desire feel pretty ambivalent about it. This ambivalence is captured in the way we commonly talk about the level of ambition a person has.

If someone were to say to you, "You have no ambition," would you take it as a compliment? Probably not. On the other hand, if someone were to say to you, "You are an ambitious person," would you take *that* as a compliment? Maybe, maybe not. How about, "You are a person of overweening personal ambition?" Now we're clearly into the realm of critique. I don't want to be called an overweening anything.

Each of us has within us a certain level of ambition that emerges from some combination of God-given attributes and the forces at work on us during our lives. However we get our level of ambition, there seems to be little we can do by force of will to change it.

It's like the fuel you buy at a gas station. Some of us have low-octane ambition pumping through our veins. You know, the 87 mark at the pump. Others of us go up the ladder to 89, 91, even 93, high-performance gasoline. A few have rocket fuel in their veins. Some of us wish for higher-octane ambition (as do our frustrated mothers, fathers, spouses, and so on), while others of us (and our loved ones) would be very glad for a lower-octane level.

I personally confess to having very high-octane ambition

coursing through my veins. It has been that way for as long as I can remember – from the time of my epic quest to become a safety patrol in fifth grade, through my unsuccessful race for student body president in sixth grade, to my thwarted desire to be a major league baseball player, and so on until today.

Many days I've been glad to have been endowed with this kind of high-octane ambition. But my personal experience and observation also teach me this: High-octane ambition is danger-ous. *The greater your level of ambition, the greater the risk that it will misdirect you, burn you, consume you, and de-stroy you – and in so doing it may destroy others.* History is littered with wreckage caused by ambitious people. Consider Alexander the Great, Napoleon, Hitler. Ambitious men all. They wanted to rule the world. Instead, the central legacy of each is, essentially, dead bodies.

The greater your level of ambition, the greater the risk that you will miss the will of God for your life and follow the dic-tates of ambition instead. Even worse – the greater your level of ambition, the greater the risk that you will be blinded even to the moral law of God. Ambition has driven many a person to do immoral things in its service. And I'm not just talking about non-Christians. Rest assured, if you have any ambition at all, it will be used to tempt you.

But I have already said that there appears to be little that can be done about the *level* of ambition one has bubbling around in the soul. This means that our main task related to ambition is to direct it to the right goals. This is one of the most difficult moral challenges faced by the Christian individual, minister, or church.

The world offers a delectable platter of goodies toward which we are invited to direct our ambition. These tasty morsels include wealth, fame, power, and privilege. Every day the media tell us in a thousand ways that we deserve such goodies and ought to direct our ambitions to getting what we deserve.

But let us not simply shake our fists at that big, bad, corrupt, tempting world that would lead us simple innocents astray. Ambition is not only out there in the world; it's in here, in the church. It cannot be disputed that the socially established churches in our country, including our own denomination, are deeply compromised by the very same worldly values.

We have structured our own life as community of faith in a way that mirrors that of the world around us. We reward rather than discourage "overweening personal ambition." We do this by giving the ambitious and successful minister greater access to increasing amounts of money, fame, power, and privilege. So it's not only the world that waves that dessert tray around. We offer our own scrumptious selection in the church.

Perhaps there is a certain inevitability about this. The church does live in the world, and the socially established church does have access to worldly goodies to reward its best and brightest for their work. But what is not inevitable and not acceptable is that we then construct a theology that blesses this worldly way of doing business and calls it Christian.

It's not like we're fooling anybody. Anyone with open eyes can see the worldly ambition operating as an effective pastor jumps every couple years from a smaller to a bigger church, gaining with each move more money, fame, power, and privilege. Isn't it interesting how God never seems to call a minister or a professor to a small institution and a smaller salary? Amazingly, God just keeps on calling all of us up the Baptist corporate ladder.

We should not congratulate ourselves for dressing up worldly ambition in superficially Christian clothing. Such transparent self-deception is the peculiar temptation of those of us in church work. We need God to deliver us.

3. Jesus and Ambition

Deliverance from mere ambition is precisely what Jesus offered the brothers Zebedee and also offers us.

James and John wanted the best seats in the house. They wanted the power, fame, privilege, and perhaps even the wealth of being the right- and left-hand men of Jesus when he came into his kingdom. The other ten didn't appreciate such overweening personal ambition. Nor did Jesus.

"Can you drink the cup I am going to drink?" Jesus asked

James and John. Glibly they assured him that they could. "You will indeed drink from my cup," Jesus said, and surely his voice was grave. For Jesus was telling them that being the right- and left-hand men of Jesus meant sharing in his agonies, drinking down with him that cup of redemptive suffering and holy sorrow to the very last dregs.

Later, when the whole bickering group gathered, Jesus taught them the place of ambition in a life spent following him. "Whoever wants to become great among you must be your servant, and whoever wants to be first must be your slave, just as the Son of Man did not come to be served, but to serve, and to give his life as a ransom for many" (Matthew 20:26-28). Just over a week later, Jesus died on the cross.

Jesus did not explicitly condemn here the desire to do something important. However, what he did say – and says to us today – is that for his followers, such ambition must be directed toward servanthood and only servanthood.

Such a redirection and channeling of ambition is the only hope for the ambitious Christian. Wealth, fame, power, privilege – Jesus says that this is what the pagans seek. Not so for those who would be his disciples. We must imitate the Son of Man and do what he did – and what he did was serve. We must serve God, our fellow Christians, and every human being.

May our Lord Jesus Christ teach us how to trade mere personal ambition for authentic Christian servanthood.

The Meaning of Marriage

Mark 10:2–9

Divorce is one of those contemporary moral issues that preachers usually avoid. From a pastoral and, dare we say it, political perspective, addressing this issue is like walking through a minefield. Yet silence is not an acceptable alternative. This 1997 sermon at Northbrook Church works at the theological framework and moral principle levels in an attempt to at least break one local church's silence on the subject. Note that I chose to address the issue positively, under the guise of marriage, rather than through a negatively oriented, full-blown treatment of divorce itself. Note also the key role of my very personal opening narrative. — dpg

Introduction

I don't really remember the day it happened. Mainly I remember the feeling I had. I was about sixteen, a basically happy suburban northern Virginia kid. We were not the Cleavers, but we were a happy family with two loving and deeply committed parents — committed, that is, both to each other and to us.

One evening Mom and Dad dropped a bombshell on us. It absolutely rocked my world. For the very first time, they told us that Dad had been married before he married Mom. It had been a miserable, wretched seven-year marriage, a mistake from the very beginning, dead through the woman's faithlessness and cruelty after a very short period of time. Yet Dad had hung in there, believing that marriage is for life and divorce is wrong, not wanting to admit he had made a terrible mistake. Finally it collapsed. A year or so later he met the woman who would become his wife and my mother. Thirty-six years after that, they still are going strong – for which I thank God.

Marriage. Divorce. Two words we know so well, yet words we infrequently hear discussed in church. Outside the context of weddings, I've never heard a sermon on either marriage or divorce. That puzzles me, and troubles me, for two reasons: (1) Marriage and divorce are significant issues in the Bible. They are addressed in several dozen passages in both Testaments and all parts of Scripture. (2) Marriage and divorce are significant issues in contemporary American society. No, that puts it way too mildly. Let me try it another way. Statistics show that marriage and family life are in the midst of a crisis unprecedented in American history. Let me share a few dismal facts with you.

1. The United States has the highest divorce rate in the entire world.

2. The median duration of a marriage in our country is 7.2 years.

3. For every two couples that get married each year, one couple will divorce.

4. The divorce rate has tripled since 1960.

5. A couple marrying today has a 60 percent chance of divorce or separation. The rates are higher if marriage is preceded by cohabitation (living together).

6. Over one million children each year experience the divorce of their parents.

7. About 40 percent of America's children live without their fathers.[1]

Do you feel sufficiently uplifted? Be of good cheer. This message is not one of gloom and doom. Indeed, I have good news, gospel news, for you today: It doesn't have to be this way. In Christ, we can do better, and many already are, including many in this room. A vital living relationship with Jesus Christ is the key to God's kind of success, in marriage and in life. Let's think about what marriage means from Scripture's perspective and how to find success in it.

The Meaning of Marriage

I want to unpack the meaning of marriage by exploring five key scriptural principles which together shape a biblical understanding of marriage. Let's dive in.

1. *Marriage is a covenant, not a contract.* A covenant is a sacred, binding, public mutual agreement between two parties. It imposes certain obligations that are freely and publicly taken on as both parties vow to do what the covenant requires. These obligations also create certain privileges for both parties. It is sacred in that its importance is seen as transcending the wishes of either individual or even of both partners – it reaches to the heavens. It is mutual and cannot work if only one person fulfills its obligations. It is binding and intended to be sturdy and lasting.

Marriage, in God's eyes, is a covenant, not a contract, and certainly not less than a contract. It is not a friendship casually taken to another level, nor is it merely a temporary joining of people who find themselves attracted to each other. You might think of it this way: A covenant is made of cement, not glue, not a rubber band, and not a paper clip.

2. *Marriage is ordained and sealed by God, not just by us.* The Bible teaches that God ordained and established marriage for his holy purposes. It's not just for us; it's also for him. And he did this in the creation before any other human institution was created or established. Marriage was the only institution created before the fall, before sin.

Jesus speaks of this same wonderful truth by saying, "What God has put together, let no one separate." Norm Geisler has put it this way: "God is the witness of all weddings, whether [he is] invited or not. Marriage is a sacred occasion whether the couple recognize it or [whether they do] not." But people don't tend to think of marriage this way anymore. They think that marriage is a private affair between "two consenting adults" who are free to enter into it for their own reasons and then free to dissolve it for their own reasons. If they invoke the name of God in their wedding service, it is merely a reflection of an old tradition. The reality, though, is that whenever marriage vows are taken, God is there, because on this earth marriage is God's business, not just ours.

3. *Marriage is exclusive, not open*. It's an interesting thing. We teach our children and each other to share, to include one another, to open the circle and let others in. And this is right — except with marriage. Marriage is the one relationship that is *supposed* to exclude people.

Now this must be understood in the right way. What it means is that there is an intimacy in marriage that is not to be shared with others. There is a zone of relating that is not to be transgressed by anyone else. Marriage, as Jesus put it, and as Genesis puts it, is a "one-flesh" relationship.

You probably think of sexual faithfulness here as I speak of this zone of intimacy, and you are right. One central area of exclusivity in marriage is sex. God is clear in his Word that he designed marriage as the exclusive forum for sexual intimacy and that this intimacy is to be shared only by the marriage partners. One of the God-given purposes of marriage is for the expression of our sexuality. Yet some have suggested in our time that this exclusivity is not really an essential part of marriage. Can you spell *recipe for disaster?*

Adultery is the fundamental violation of this zone of intimacy. But it is not the only one, and there are forms of "adultery" that do not involve actual physical conduct. Fidelity in sexuality is a matter of the mind and of the heart, not just the body.

Also, we have to talk about exclusivity in terms of other kinds of intimacy. Jeanie and I knew a couple whose marriage was deeply troubled. The wife in this marriage after a while developed a close, intimate, but nonsexual friendship with another man. It was soon clear to us that the level of intimacy was closer with this other man than with her husband. This always spells trouble for a marriage. And, sure enough, it was not many years before she ended her marriage and married the other man. Intimacy boundaries must be guarded even if there is no intimation of sexual attraction, for fidelity in intimacy is also a matter of the heart.

4. *Marriage is a mutual partnership, not a forum for meeting my needs only*. "It is not good for the man to be alone,"

God noted in the Garden of Eden; "I will make a helper suitable for him." Some translations have "partner" in place of "helper." Perhaps the fundamental purpose of marriage, from God's perspective, is partnership. God cares about relationships. He is involved within his own majestic person in a Father-Son-Spirit relationship. He wants us to enjoy the overflow of that relational unity and intimacy, and he has made us people who seek such a relationship. No one has to tell us to look for a bone-of-bone, flesh-of-flesh partner. We do it naturally. And when we find such a person — as I can personally attest — we reach levels of joy that can hardly be paralleled by any other aspect of human life.

But this cannot happen unless the marriage is truly a mutual partnership. Marriage works when spouses seek to meet each other's needs above all else. Thus, both partners' needs are met and, mysteriously, in losing their lives, they find them.

I once talked with a woman who said, "I've been married twice, and in both marriages I gave 95 percent and my husband gave 5 percent." Men, women, that will not do. We must both do our part or the entire enterprise will be threatened with disaster. We must do our part in raising the kids, in doing household chores, in communicating, in resolving conflicts, in providing a good spiritual climate for the home, and so on.

5. *Marriage is permanent, not temporary.* Jesus said, "What God has joined together, let no one separate." Well, there you have it; it's as easy as that, right?

Then there's Liz Taylor, who's on her seventh husband, I think. And there's the nationally known talk-show host, Larry King, who is about to marry again and who has said publicly that each wife was the right one for each particular stage of his life, and thus there was nothing wrong with all these marriages and divorces.

God doesn't see it that way. Jesus doesn't either. The Pharisees came to him and asked him to tell them if it is "lawful" — acceptable according to Jewish law — for a man to divorce his wife. In Matthew, in the parallel passage, the question is not whether divorce is okay, but whether it is okay "for any cause," meaning, "What are the legitimate grounds for divorce?"

You have to understand the context at the time. In Jewish

culture, divorce was easily available – to men, that is – women could not obtain a divorce. The rule was that a man had to write out a certificate of divorce that basically said, "I divorce you and you are free to marry someone else." He gave this to his ex-wife as he booted her out the door.

The rabbis debated when such an action might be lawful. The strict rabbis said that divorce was okay only if a woman misbehaved sexually. The more lenient school said divorce was okay for any reason a man might have, such as bad cooking or even the availability of a more beautiful woman. The practice at the time leaned in the direction of wide-open divorce – much like today.

Jesus turned the question around. He didn't want to engage the Pharisees in a conversation on those terms. He didn't want to play the lawyer. He wanted to say what God intends: Marriage is permanent. Don't break it up. Cleave to one another for life.

In another sermon on another day I could talk about possible last-resort exceptions to that rule. Christian opinion is divided as to what exceptions might be legitimate. In Matthew, Jesus says that adultery would be a legitimate exception. Paul, in 1 Corinthians, concedes that an unbeliever deserting his Christian spouse can be a legitimate reason for divorce. I personally think that situations of physical abuse or grossly immoral living or endangerment to the children or other such fundamental offenses against the marriage covenant might qualify as legitimate. But that's not what we're supposed to emphasize. Marriage is permanent. Divorce is at best a last-resort concession to sin and one that frequently creates as many problems as it solves.

Conclusion

If we believe these principles, and more important, if we live them – we will be very, very different from our culture. Indeed, I am convinced that the only way we can either believe or live this is if we are absolutely committed to following the way of Christ rather than the way of the world. And by "we" I don't

just mean "we" the individuals gathered here or "we" the couples gathered here – I mean "we" the community of faith. For
together we can and must uphold each other's marriages and
protect each other's families.

If you are seeking to know what Christianity is about this
day, you've come on a good day. Christianity is about living the
way God designed – beginning wherever you are right now. It's
about knowing what that way is and having a strong, tough-
minded, and committed group of people around you who also
know the way and are committed to living it. And it's about the
wonder and joy of life lived in the midst of this people and in
the way God designed. What a glorious privilege!

NOTE

1. U.S. Government, *Statistical Abstract of the United States 1997*
and William Bennett, *The Index of Leading Cultural Indicators* (New
York: Simon & Shuster, 1994).

Off the Barrel's Bottom
Mark 12:41–44

This sermon was originally designed as a morally focused message on the issue of the proper handling of money. The terrible spring 1997 floods that hit our area provided a painful but profound context in which to offer these reflections. This sermon is aimed primarily at the Christian and works largely at the theological framework level. — rhl

We are such an affluent and comfortable society that we have become numb to suffering. An ever-growing callus covers our hearts and our sensibilities where the suffering and pain and tragedy of others is concerned. Therefore, it takes a great deal to shock us. It takes much to cause us to look at others and sense a little bit of what they are going through. Yet when we look back over the events of the last week, we are reminded that our hearts are probably not as hard as we tended to think in our most self-critical moments. When you begin to put together names and faces, people you know in this community, streets where you have walked, and you see them now completely inundated by flood waters, the heartache begins to touch you. You know some of those folks. And you know some of the pain, sorrow, and loss they are going through.

But life, like a flood, has a way of enveloping us so that what we are feeling in one moment is swept away in the next. Before long, you and I both know that will happen. As the flood waters recede and the Ohio finds its way back into its banks, we will go on with our lives and forget what we could have and should have learned during this process. We will get so busy in living that we will put it aside, and if it did not directly impact us, we will forget about it. So while it is still fresh on our minds, like an open wound, I want us to go back into Scripture and find a lesson that we should all learn together. It is a lesson about who owns what. This past week we have been reminded that the earth still is the Lord's. And you and I don't own nearly as much as we claim we do.

Several years ago I was the pastor of a small county seat town in extreme western Kentucky. If you went much farther west, you had to swim across the Mississippi River, and then when you climbed out of its banks, you broke through a tree line and very soon after crossing that tree line, you went into some of the most marvelous flat prairie farmland you will ever see, just inside Missouri. And if you looked across the western sky, all you could see was unbroken prairie except for the dots of the utility poles and breaks that marked the county roads and an occasional tree that had been planted out there. Otherwise, it was an unending flat for as far as the eye could see. Five generations of folks in the same family had owned that land. But, if you will remember, in the early 1980s farming in America went through a tremendous upheaval. Farmers had been encouraged to borrow much more than was probably good for them on the understanding that crop prices were just going to continue to go up, and so when the bottom fell out of the grain prices, many of those same farmers had their farms in danger of being repossessed by the very government that had loaned them the money to begin with.

I will never forget the story of the man whose family had owned that particular farm for five generations. One day he walked out across the ground he loved so much and stood in the middle of a field. There he put a gun to his head and ended his life. And the ground that he claimed he owned absorbed his blood and shed not one tear for his passing. Not one. All this because a piece of paper had come in his mailbox saying that another piece of paper he had in his safe deposit box was no longer valid. But he really never did own that land; he merely occupied it for a period of time. It was given to him as a trust for a period of time, and then he would give it back.

This morning I want you to understand that you and I are not owners. As children of God, as Christians, we are stewards, managers. Land, property, money, and resources are all God's. We manage those things on his behalf and under his direction. And at some point we will give back everything we claim to own. The New Testament says that Christians should recognize this and live our lives accordingly. But the sad truth of the matter is that most of us don't live that way at all. We act like we are owners. We act like everything we can gather around us is ours to do with as we please. And when something happens to place in danger that which we claim we own, we sometimes react violently. Sometimes we act with a sense of resignation. Seldom do we act as children of God should. But if you want to see how we ought to live, look at the snapshot in this story found in Mark's Gospel.

Now let's set the scene. Jesus has triumphantly entered Jerusalem on what we celebrate as Palm Sunday. Every day he goes to the temple area. There is a particular court inside the temple compound where Jewish men gather around rabbis and scholars of the law and debate technical points of the law. They debate theology and its impact on their lives, and those debates go on endlessly, hour after hour. Jesus has been there debating with the scribes and Pharisees, the teachers of the law. One of the challenges they put before him is found in Mark 11, in those last few verses, when Jesus enters. The first thing they say to him is, "By whose authority do you teach?" So the whole issue from that portion of Mark 11 on through what we have read today is the issue of authority.

Jesus looks at the religious leaders and says (my paraphrase): "You are much more dangerous than you appear. For your worship is so elaborate. It is so profound. You make such pretense about how you worship God. But your lives have this horrible disconnection between the way you have professed to live and the way you actually live. And that makes you dangerous." If our Lord were here today and in many other churches across America, what he would say to us would be a similar indictment. It is one thing for us to elaborately worship God, but if there is no connection between the way we worship God and the way we live, we are dangerous.

After Jesus' confrontation with the religious leaders, he walks over into another court, the Court of Women. Women and gentiles were segregated away from most of the temple compound. In this court, where the women and gentiles could come, there were thirteen receptacles built into the wall. They were trumpet-shaped, made of brass, and they were built into the wall. It was there that people came and placed their offerings. All day long, men and women from all walks of life would come and drop their offering into one of those thirteen receptacles. Surely there were those who came up and were heralded in their approach by the ruffling of their grand finery. These wealthy people would drop their offering in and everyone would take notice.

If you don't believe that human nature looks at those things, let me tell you a story about something that happened to me. A few years ago the Southern Baptist Convention, for some unknown reason, decided that they would go to Las Vegas. You have never lived until you have seen about thirty thousand Baptist preachers trying to figure out how they are going to play a slot machine without anybody at home finding out. A friend of mine and I went to Caesar's Palace one night. We were staying in a different hotel, but I had heard of Caesar's Palace for years and wanted to see it. When we walked into Caesar's Palace, we saw more political figures and public figures than I had ever seen in one place before. Professional athletes were all over the place. Over in the corner, roped off by velvet ropes, were slot machines. Nobody was playing them until one guy, wearing a beat-up cowboy hat and little string tie, walked back there. Suddenly everybody around stopped what they were doing and watched. The man took out three huge coins and plugged them into that slot machine. He pulled the arm and then shrugged his shoulders and walked away empty-handed. I didn't know what it meant, so I asked somebody what had happened. Why had everybody stopped? I found out that each of those coins was worth $500. He had put $1,500 in a slot machine and come up empty.

Can't you imagine people in the temple court stopping to watch when prominent figures approach one of the receptacles to put in their offering? But probably nearly no one notices when a widow comes by with her meager offering. She drops two coins into one of the receptacles. But Jesus, who is leaning against the wall, sees her. He gathers his disciples to him and says, "Now there's an offering!" Scripture says the widow gave her entire estate, everything she had. Do you know that if you were to take the equivalency rates of those coins and multiply them out, she gave less than one-twentieth of an average worker's weekly wages? That is all she had — two coins. And that is what she put in.

I want you to understand that when we talk about stewardship we are not talking only about money. That is the least important issue in stewardship. We are talking about a way of life, about how you live your life as a child of God. You see, we are supposed to live our lives as managers, as stewards. And if we do not live that way, everything we claim about God has this horrible sense of being disconnected from the way we actually live. Too many of us proclaim God's greatness in our worship and songs and prayers while we are in church and then live a life that denies everything we claim we believe about God.

The widow in our text shows us how we ought to live. The first thing she teaches us is that stewardship is an attitude long before it is ever an action. And in doing so, all she does is teach us exactly what Jesus also taught. Do you remember the passage of Scripture that makes every man smile a nervous little smile, the one when Jesus is talking about what constitutes adultery? The law as interpreted by the rabbis was very precise and very technical. It said that adultery was committed when a married man took to his bed someone other than his wife. But Jesus said, "Oh no, that's not it." Like every other choice in a Christian's behavior, adultery is an attitude before it is ever an action. If a man looks at another woman and lusts, he is guilty. All of us need to understand that the choices we make in life, the attitudes we have, are where we begin to demonstrate exactly what we truly believe about God. Stewardship is an attitude long before it is ever an action. What kind of attitude is it? Well, if you look at that little woman long enough, and you watch her silently pay tribute to God's grace and glory, you discover that stewardship reflects our confidence in God rather than our financial standing.

The Bible says a great deal about the widow. In a society where women were looked down upon for the most part, widows had virtually nothing to fall back on. If her deceased husband had a brother and if by this time they were still holding to the strict letter of the law, it would have been her dead husband's brother's responsibility to take care of her. But many times there was no brother or, if there were, he simply did not live up to his obligation.

You might ask, "Where were her sons and daughters? Why didn't they take care of her?" We don't know where they were. Perhaps that marriage was never blessed with children. But it could very well have been that they were well off and had high standing in the community. Some children, instead of caring for their aging parents as they were biblically obligated to do, simply declared everything they possessed to be dedicated to God. This way they could "dedicate" all they had to God and still keep it and use it for their own benefit, thus worming their way out of their obligations to those for whom they should have been caring.

We don't really know the widow's situation, but those who could have taken care of her either did not exist or chose to turn their backs on her. As a result, everything she had fit in the palm of her hand. If ever there was someone who had the right to ask, "God, why have you done me this way? Can't you do something to help me?" it is this widow. Yet she doesn't do anything that you and I might do. She demonstrates a silent confidence in God that cries out volumes as we read this text. She says by her actions that we can have confidence in God when we recognize that everything is his. This woman knew more about God and God's grace than many of us will ever know. Why? Because she took everything she possessed and in one motion of her hand tossed it into that receptacle to say, "I trust in God." In that one act, she preached more sermons than most preachers will ever preach. She gave more witness – and a much more credible witness – than many of us will ever vocalize. And if no one else in that temple noticed what she did, Jesus noticed. He called his disciples over and said, "Now you have seen something that is incredibly powerful."

You see, stewardship is not what you choose to do with your money. It is the attitude you should live your life by if you are a child of God. Stewardship is the very philosophy upon which your life should be built. It is an attitude before it is ever an action. And it is an attitude that demonstrates and reflects a growing confidence in God – not your financial standing, not your social status, not anything else about you. Think of all the ways we choose to measure ourselves to determine whether we have worth. This woman demonstrated incredible worth when she proved her trust in God in the most tangible of ways – by giving everything she had.

Finally, stewardship is the truest marker of the direction of your worship. It is true that worship happens when we gather here corporately from Sunday to Sunday. And it is something that, when it works as it is intended to, is a beautiful, powerful testimony to our community. Our only common bond is Jesus Christ and our love and commitment to him. Yet that is enough for us to share each other's sorrows. When you are weak and I have a strength, you can draw from my strength. And when I am weak and you are strong, I can draw from your strength. We can share those moments together, and that is what corporate worship is supposed to be. But there is also another kind of worship – the kind you do privately in the midnight of your soul, when you are alone with God. In the midnight of this widow's soul, she is the truest witness you will find of God's grace, power, love, and care.

I have heard a lot of testimonies behind pulpits in twenty-plus years of being a pastor. I have heard all kinds of statements made about God, but there is nothing quite as winsome, nothing quite as powerful as somebody whose life points out for you the true direction of their worship. The widow was saying in what she did that God is worthy of my absolute confidence and trust. God is worthy. Now let me be blunt. Some of you here today would have to say, "I would love to know that I didn't have to manage things on my own. But I am not a Christian. What do I do?" Well, if you choose not to be a Christian, you do the best you can. I'm not trying to be flippant. That is about all I know to tell you. And if you are smart enough and focused enough, you can hold on to what you have for a little while. But you are going to lose in the end. I'm sorry to tell you, but you are going to lose. And that is sad. You know what is sadder? Watching some Christians act like owners instead of stewards. Today why don't you say that regardless of your place in life, "I just want to put this burden down and rest. I surrender." May God give you the grace and courage to do just that.

Hearing God's Voice
in a New Museum
Luke 10:25–37

This sermon was offered in a unique and very precious setting: Providence Baptist Church of McLean, Virginia, my first church home as a new Christian believer. It was also offered at a unique, kairos *kind of moment: the time of the opening of the United States Holocaust Museum, just up the road from Providence Church in our nation's capital. This 1993 sermon brings together two narratives — one biblical (the story of the good Samaritan), and the other historical (the story of the Holocaust). It is an attempt to provide moral instruction to Christian people through reflection on altruistic behavior, and its lack, in the midst of human suffering. — dpg*

Introduction

If you have been reading the newspapers or watching the news this week, you know that three days ago President Clinton dedicated the United States Holocaust Memorial Museum at a site just off the Mall in the monumental heart of Washington and the nation. Tomorrow, at 10 A.M., this unique monument to human evil and memorial of human suffering will open to the public.

For the past three years, I've been writing my dissertation about the Holocaust. The Holocaust was the mass murder of six million Jews and five million other civilians by Nazi Germany during World War II. My field is Christian ethics – the exploration of what it means to live like a Christian, to follow Jesus in every aspect of one's life. I've studied the Holocaust because there we see *the negation of every decent human impulse and every principle of authentic Christian ethics.* I've wanted to know how people who drank Christian faith with their mother's milk could have grown up to shoot, gas, and burn millions of innocent men, women, and children. It's an effort to learn from the failure of Christians and Christian culture. Just as we can and do hear God's voice in our moments of triumph, goodness, and obedience to God, so we too can hear God's voice in our moments of failure, evil, and disobedience. By placing the Holocaust Museum in the same place as happier monuments like the Jefferson Memorial and the Washington Monument, our nation is doing the same thing: trying to learn from the worst as well as the best. And so we begin, seeking to hear God's voice in the Holocaust (of all places) and in the strange and disturbing new museum that now stands on the Washington Mall.

Participants in the Holocaust Drama

When you visit the Holocaust Museum, you'll encounter four different kinds of people – that is, people in four different kinds of roles. They are: (1) perpetrators – those who performed the deeds of murder; (2) victims – those who died at the hands of the perpetrators; (3) bystanders – those who neither killed nor were killed but "stood by" and did nothing; and (4) rescuers – that tiny minority of bystanders who stopped "standing by" and instead risked their lives to help Jews.

We see the same four groups of people in our New Testament reading this morning. One of the great things about Jesus' teaching is the way his stories reveal truths about the human situation that are true for all times and places. Let's talk about perpetrators, victims, bystanders, and rescuers in the Good Samaritan story and in the Holocaust. Let's see if we can hear God's voice.

Perpetrators

> Luke 10:30 – "A man...fell into the hands of robbers. They stripped him of his clothes, beat him, and went away, leaving him half dead."

> Holocaust – "Eleven million people fell into the hands of robbers and murderers. They stripped these people of their rights, their place in society, their possessions, and finally, of their lives."

What can be said about perpetrators? Is there a word from God? There is much to say, but at least these things:

1. *We were made for better.* "God saw all that he had made, and it was very good" (Genesis 1:31). God made us with such care, but why? So that we could love him and love our neighbors with whom we share this earth, God's garden. God had great dreams for us, and he still does. Sometimes, by God's grace, we treat other people with the care and respect each of God's creatures deserves. Too often, we do not. When we pierce the flesh of our neighbors with weapons, we do not.

2. *God grieves over us.* Do you remember this text from Genesis 6:5–6: "The LORD saw how great man's wickedness on the earth had become,...The LORD was grieved that he had made man on the earth, and his heart was filled with pain"? Every time human beings die at the hands of others, God grieves again.

3. *We go wrong in so many ways.* In the Good Samaritan story, the robbers' motives are not spelled out. We assume they wanted the man's clothes, money, and other belongings. But why beat him half dead? Was that necessary? Do we see sadism here – the joy of inflicting pain for pain's sake? In the Holocaust, we see the same thing. Motives as basic as greed – the desire to get Jews' possessions – and as evil as sadism.

But in the Holocaust we also see other paths to wrongdoing, ones less remote to us, more of a danger. We see people "following orders" no matter how evil those orders. We see people doing the worst things because they love their country. We see the fear of consequences: "If I don't carry out this order, what will happen to me?" We see careerism and ambition as we watch bright young men and women enter the Nazi SS so they can make their way to the top of their society.

There are so many ways to go wrong. Some are pure evil, and anyone could tell you so. Others are seemingly reasonable motives that lead to disaster. Can anyone deny the depths of our sin? Or of our need for a Redeemer and Lord?

Victims

> Luke 10:30 – "A man was going down from Jerusalem to Jericho, when he fell into the hands of robbers."

> Holocaust – "Jews and other people were living out their normal lives in Europe, and they fell into the hands of murderers."

Jesus helps us to imagine a man just going about his business, taking a routine trip on a routine day. Just like any of us going to the grocery story, the mall, or down I-95. And then in a horrible moment, his life is changed forever. Whatever he was – rich or poor, husband or single, father or childless – dissolves and he becomes a stripped-naked and bleeding human being who needs help to survive.

The same thing was true in the Holocaust. In the museum you'll see people just like yourself: men, women, children, rich, poor, fathers, mothers, daughters, sons, scholars, housewives, farmers, bookkeepers. And then they fell among robbers. . . .

Can we hear God's voice in the anguish of the victims? I think so. At least these truths are evident:

1. *Victims do not deserve their fate, nor does God will it.* Victims are a result of a perpetrator's sin, not any fault of their own. God's will is that his creatures stop victimizing others.

2. *God identifies with victims, not perpetrators.* Our God is a God whose heart burns with sorrow when people are turned into victims. We also see the extent of God's identification with victims on the cross, when the spotless and sinless Lamb of God was slain.

3. *God calls us to help victims.* In the Holocaust Museum you will see pictures, both of happy, smiling Jewish mothers, fathers, and children before the war and then of the victims the Nazis made. God's call then was the same as it is now: Whenever you can, prevent people from being turned into victims.

Bystanders

Luke 10:31-32 – "A priest happened to be going down the same road, and when he saw the man, he passed by on the other side. So too, a Levite...."

Holocaust – "Millions of local European non-Jews, and (by and large) the world community...saw the victims, and passed by the other side."

The import of the story of the Good Samaritan really begins to be felt when Jesus tells of the two religious leaders – a priest and a Levite – who saw the victim and yet passed by on the other side. How could they do such a thing?

We don't know, really. Perhaps they were frightened that the man might be pretending, that the robbers might be nearby, and that one or both might do the same to them. Perhaps they did not want to break certain ritual requirements that related to their official religious positions – touching the dead defiled the priest, for example. Perhaps they were late for appointments and couldn't find the time. Or perhaps they simply didn't care.

My research has revealed that most European Christians were bystanders to the Holocaust. A small minority actively became involved in killing Jews. Another small minority risked their lives to help Jews survive. The great majority were bystanders, neither harming nor helping, staying out of it altogether.

What can God be saying through the bystanders?

1. *Being a bystander is the refuge of the decent majority*. Most of us feel a spark of sympathy for others in need. This is a gift from God to us. But many things can block us from acting on it, so most of us remain bystanders. Nurture that compassion, and resist all forces that act on it.

2. *Being a bystander is not enough*. The priest and Levite didn't hurt the man, but neither did they help him. It was not enough; if everyone had done the same, he would have died on the road. Evil must be met by active goodness, human need by active compassion, hatred by active love. As Edmund Burke said, "All that is required for evil to prevail is for good men to do nothing."

Rescuers

Luke 10:33–34 – "But a Samaritan, as he traveled, came where the man was; and when he saw him, he took pity on him. He went to him and bandaged his wounds."

Holocaust – "But some Christians, when they saw the plight of the Jews, took pity on them. They went to Jews and hid them in their homes, rescued them from ghettos, bandaged their wounds, and helped them survive the war."

On the basement level of the Holocaust Museum – after you have traced the course of the Holocaust and seen the worst that humans can do – you will see a tribute to those who rescued Jews during the Holocaust. You'll see a boat from Denmark, one of the hundreds that were used to smuggle almost all of that nation's Jews to Sweden – and to safety. You'll see the well-worn Bible of Pastor Andre Trocme, leader of a French town that hid five thousand Jews. And you'll see some of the safe-conduct passes that the famed Swedish diplomat Raoul Wallenberg used to save one hundred thousand Hungarian Jews in 1944.

In Jesus' tale we meet a person who refuses either to beat a man when he's down or to pass by on the other side. He acts on his pity and does the simple things that are needed: bandaging, carrying the victim away, finding lodging, making financial provisions. He used the resources available to him and did what he could. So did those who rescued Jews during the Holocaust. Both overcame their fears and did what they could to help.

What might God be saying here in Luke, and in the basement of the Holocaust Museum?

1. *Goodness is possible even in the most profoundly evil contexts; compassion is possible even when it is risky*. Was it true that "nothing could be done" to help Jews, as so many Europeans said after the war? No, the actions of some one hundred thousand European rescuers tell a different story. Almost always something can be done to prevent harm or to ease the plight of victims. Even now.

2. *Goodness and compassion must be practiced concretely*. We can do such basic things as feeding, washing, financing, carrying, arranging, and so on. It doesn't take an expert – not a Ph.D., for heaven's sake – just a caring heart and active hands.

3. *This is what Jesus did in life and in death, and what those who strive to follow him must do as well.*

Dear Lord, may our hands be active and kind so that we can help others; may our feet be swift to go to those in need; may our hearts be brave to face risks to ourselves so that we can do your work in the world. Help us to be good neighbors to those we see along the roadway of our lives. Empower us by your Spirit to be your hands, feet, and heart in the world. Amen.

Call Me Back
When the Party's Over

Luke 15:11–32

This 1997 sermon moves in the direction of being expository in form. Its text, the Prodigal Son story, is a familiar one. Here I tried to draw some of the moral implications of the story to go along with the more typically addressed theological issues. —rhl

When people give up reality to live in a fantasy world, we say that they need to seek professional help. That is, we say that in practically every area of life except one – pleasure seeking. We really do let people off the hook when they say, "Excuse me, I don't want to stay in the real world. I would much prefer to play in my fantasy world."

Pleasure is a multibillion-dollar industry. In fact, we spend more money on our play than on perhaps any other aspect of our lives. It is that important to us. But we need to understand that how we seek pleasure and how we distance ourselves from the real world often have a narcotic-like effect on us. After a while the fix just isn't good enough. We have to go back for more and more and more. Now, I understand that playing is important. It is part of what it means to be human and part of a human culture. Someone has suggested that the more complex and sophisticated the culture, the more the need for play.

But when we spend all of our time seeking pleasure, avoiding reality, that is not normal. In fact, it is dangerous. And the real trouble is that so many people who today are engaged in their play, in their pleasure, wouldn't think of coming here or to a place like this because they don't want to talk about

God. They don't want to talk about their needs. They don't really want to talk about who they are. They are too busy being caught up in their play. It is as if they are saying to us collectively this morning, "Leave me alone and let me do what I want to do. And after my party is over, then perhaps we will talk about God." This is not just an American phenomenon; it is as old as humanity itself.

Jesus used that same concept to give us one of the most beautiful of all his parables, the story of the Prodigal Son. You remember the story from your childhood if you grew up anywhere near a church. It is actually one of a set of three parables that Jesus teaches in this section of the book of Luke. All three parables teach essentially the same theological truth – that God is a loving God who yearns to have a personal relationship with you, who wants to be connected to you, and who takes the initiative to make that connection.

I want us to go back and think again about this familiar story. There was this father who had two sons. One day, for some reason, the younger of the two sons comes to his father and says, "I want what is mine now." The first thing we think of is the audacity of this boy. How in the world would anybody have the gall to walk up to Dad and say, "Dad, I want my part now"? Actually, Hebrew law allowed for such an occurrence. You see, if the father chose to have his estate disbursed after his death, the law was quite specific: Two-thirds of all that he owned would go to the oldest son, and all the rest that he possessed would be divided in other ways. If the father, for whatever reason, wanted to do something different, he had to give his property away prior to his death, because once he died, the law kicked in. So occasionally individuals would come along and do just that. They would take their capital goods and give them to their heirs before their death. Generally they kept the income that might be produced from that capital for the rest of their lives. But actual ownership was transferred.

Once the man had given away his property, he could never sell it, because it had in fact been given away. Interestingly enough, if he gave it to you, you could sell it or could write a contract to sell it. But you couldn't execute the contract until the original owner died. Then you were free to do with your property, now fully in your possession, whatever you chose to do. It was not an uncommon occurrence, and that is why Jesus used it as the basis of the story. What is fairly uncommon — though it did occasionally happen — was for the heir to come and say, "I'm going to take mine now and do what I want with it." In the parable the boy decides at some later time that he is going to strike out on his own. Though it is probably unwise for us to make too much of this, the story is couched in such a way that most likely this boy has decided he is going to shake the dust of his crummy little home country off his feet and is going to make his fortune. He is going to kiss his past goodbye and make a new life for himself. And off he goes.

There is just one problem with his plan: The money is burning a hole in his pocket. Once he gets to another place, he probably thinks, *I'm going to spend a little of this now and enjoy it. Then I am going to really roll up my sleeves and get busy.* Maybe he thinks, *I'm going to have one wild fling — a real good party — because after that I'm just going to have to put my nose to the grindstone.* The problem is, he and his companions who are there to help him make sure he spends his money don't know when to quit. Eventually two problems crop up in this boy's life. The first one he creates. The second one just happens. Bad luck. Bad timing. Bad something. Not his fault.

The first problem is that he has spent and spent and spent until he has nothing left to spend. That is his fault. The next problem is just unfortunate. At the same time that his pockets run dry, a famine hits the land. All of a sudden he looks around, and all those people who were there for him when he was bankrolling the party are gone. Our hero is in serious trouble. All of his plans have been derailed. Eventually it gets so bad that he does what no one from his country would ever do: He goes to a hog farmer and decides to take whatever job is available. He ends up out in a field somewhere away from everyone. The good life is gone, and he is wondering how he got there as he is looking for something to eat.

Pods grew on a type of tree that was indigenous to that region. Extremely poor people would steam them and eat the gooey substance inside. It had no nutritional value whatsoever, but it was very filling. This is the same thing the Bible seems to be describing as the food the hogs were eating. That is all the prodigal has. The good life is long gone, and he is hurting. The party is over, and he feels like he has been left out. There are some lessons that he learns that you and I need to know. I am convinced that every one of us in this room who seriously wants a connection to God knows someone who is saying, "I don't have time for that God business. Leave me alone. I'm enjoying my life. Come see me when my party is over." It's hard to build a bridge to get such people to talk to you.

I remember a friend of mine from college. I was trying to describe to him the confidence, peace, serenity, and joy that I found in my relationship with Christ. He kept hearing that somehow I was supposed to do a lot of things that religious people did and not do things that religious people avoided. He heard rules and regulations every time I said faith and serenity and peace. I kept wanting him to say, "I want to hear about this Jesus that you talk about." He kept saying, "I don't want to talk about God. I'm too busy with my party. Life is one unending pleasure. I'll talk to you when it's over." A lot of us know someone like that, and most of us at some point in our lives, perhaps even now, have been that someone.

The prodigal learned some lessons in the far country, and if we're smart, we will learn from them. The first lesson he learned is that life is tougher than you have resources to manage. You don't start out trying to fail, do you? It is a rare person who sets out saying, "You know, failure is not a bad thing. I think I'll give it a shot. If I fail, I fail. In fact, I half way expect I will, and it doesn't bother me." This young man didn't start out to fail; he got caught up in looking for pleasure and avoiding pain, and he found out that life outlasted his resources.

You see, there were two resources that he was going to depend on, and he figured that he had enough of both so that he would be able to take care of himself. He figured first of all that his pocket was deep enough to get him through. He thought he would always have enough money to manage life. He also figured that if for some reason he was no longer liquid in his financial condition, he had friends enough that he could call on. And who knows, maybe if that famine hadn't come along, he would have been in good shape. Maybe his pockets would have been deep enough. Maybe if he had kept a little bit of money back, he would have been able to withstand or outlast the famine. Bad luck, bad timing, bad something – we don't know. But what we do know is this: He offers a painful lesson not just for himself but for all of us. Life will outlast our resources, and there are just way too many of us who don't want to have anything to do with God because we are so busy trying to make sure we cover our bases. While we search out our pleasures, we avoid any contact with pain. We don't want to have any of that. We believe we have enough resources available to us on our own to take care of whatever comes our way. It is a bad choice. A very, very bad choice.

The second lesson this young man learned is that the party ends in disillusionment. Verse 17 of the passage arrests our attention: "When he came to his senses." There is a point here at which absolute disillusionment sets in. He wakes up, sobers up, comes to himself. After the party is over, all he has left is disillusionment. Those people you care about who are saying, "I don't want to hear about your God and your faith or any of that stuff. I don't want any of that for my life right now," are essentially failing to see that eventually every party runs out and ends in disillusionment.

Have you ever really seen a drug addict? I saw a man several years ago in Memphis who shattered my illusion about drug addicts. I once had a mental picture of drug addicts that placed them in a class below me. But then I had an experience in Memphis. I was with a friend of mine who managed a shelter for alcoholics and drug abusers in north Memphis. There was a mission downtown on Union Street, and you could go there to get a hot meal and to sleep. But if you were serious about getting your life back on track, you went out to north Memphis to this place where you could dry out. I'll never forget one gentleman I met. He looked just exactly like what I thought a drug addict ought to look like. He was dirty, disheveled, and needed to shave. He smelled like body odor. I just figured, *Well, there is nothing to this guy*. At least that's what I thought until I was told by my friend that I was standing in front of a board-certified, licensed medical doctor. He didn't start out that way. He ended that way in disillusionment.

They tell me that if you put a frog in scalding hot water, the first instinct of that frog is to jump out. But if you put that same frog in water that is room temperature and then slowly begin to increase the temperature, the frog will sit there and be slowly boiled to death because it does not understand what is happening. I look at people every day who remind me of that frog. They are boiling their lives away, seeking their pleasures, trying to avoid pain, yet in the process they are compounding pain after pain on top of their lives.

The young man in our parable learned a high-priced lesson, a lesson far more costly than all of the money that had poured out of his pocket originally. He had to look at what was left of his life as he came to his senses. The party was over, and he had to see what he was. America has one of the highest suicide rates in all of the civilized world, and a significant part of that is because men and women are waking up from all of the parties they are living in, all their pleasure seeking, and looking at what is left. They can't stand to see what is there. Folks, those are the people who live next door to you and around the corner from you and sometimes in the house with you.

But the last lesson is the most important. The boy discovers that the father's love has never been removed. Everyone who heard Jesus tell this story and anyone who reads it as it is printed for us in Luke understands that the father is a beautiful, simple, powerful image of God. The boy had every right to see himself as worthless. He is not just wallowing in self-pity when he says, "I think I can't be a son anymore." You have to understand what he has done. He has taken every tangible connection that he had to his father and wasted it. He hasn't had any communication with his father as far as we know. He doesn't know what his father thinks. But he does know that though his father may no longer receive him as a son, his father's character can be trusted. So he is going to go and throw himself upon the mercy of the father. What he wants to do is to become a hired hand on his father's farm.

Jesus teaches us in this story that God's love has never left us. I don't know why or how, but when God looked at you and thought of spending eternity without you, it was more than he was willing to accept. His love for you is absolutely that great.

You and I look in the mirror after the party is over and recognize that we have wasted so much. God looks at us and says that an eternity without us is absolutely intolerable. So he finds a way to connect with us. Most of us are pretty messed up. The party has left us in a heap. So God is going to have to find a way to reach us.

The Bible says that Jesus is the bridge that God chooses to use to let you and me — disheveled, disillusioned, dirty, filthy — come into the presence of the holy God. Do you know what the irony is? The people who are looking for that party and keep saying to you and me and everyone else that they just don't have time for God because they are searching for a way to magnify their pleasure and avoid their pain tend to end up with the thing they try to avoid because they turn their backs on the one sure outlet that exists for real meaning and ultimate joy. Those who are searching for God have a decision to make. We have to mirror that decision in our lives every day. It is a decision that says, "I am not a Christian because I have to be. I am a Christian because I choose to be. I'd rather have Jesus."

From Isolation to Community
John 15:12–17

This 1997 sermon was part of an emphasis on our congregation's core values at the time of the resignation of our lead pastor. This is "moral" exhortation at the broadest level — it might even be called pre-moral. Yet the focus on accountable Christian community is indispensable for discussion of any particular moral issue and for the nurture of a morally mature community of believers. This sermon is targeted to the local congregation, in this case Northbrook Church, and to the individuals who stand at varying points in relation to it. — dpg

I became a Christian at the relatively late age of sixteen. My first really good Christian friend was a newcomer in my high school whom I will call Bill. Bill was a State Department kid whose last stop had been in Central America. He was a deeply committed believer. We became inseparable. We led a Bible study together for a number of kids in our high school, attended a weekly Christian leader prayer breakfast, held each other accountable to avoid the evangelistic dating syndrome, and so on. He was my best friend.

We managed to swing it to go to the same college and even to room together. We started a two-dorm Bible study that attracted dozens of people at our very secular college. I remember one open-air September Bible study that filled the courtyard.

During our sophomore year our relationship began to change. I fell hard for a girl I shouldn't have been dating; he fell hard for secular philosophy and for heavy metal — his favorite group was AC/DC. He began having serious doubts about

Christianity and after a while renounced his commitment and stopped going to church. Instead, he stayed home reading philosophy, smoking his pipe, and listening to AC/DC. I knew we were in trouble when one day I came home from class and put on my syrupy Evie tape. About halfway through an amazingly sweet song I heard a new addition – Bill had taped over Evie with AC/DC's "Highway to Hell." It made for quite a contrast, as you might imagine.

Our relationship never recovered. Bill never came back to the faith, at least that I know about. My richest experience of Christian community had been lost.

Our church's fourth "official core value" is this: Relationships of integrity and compassion provide the best context for life change. I believe that. And so this is the point I will seek to make in a variety of ways this morning: *Christ calls us to move from isolation into meaningful relationships of Christian community.* It is a very difficult thing to do. Let's begin by trying to understand why.

1. *We live in a society that fosters isolation rather than community.* In their landmark 1985 book, *Habits of the Heart: Individualism and Commitment in American Life,* Robert Bellah and a team of researchers talked with hundreds of Americans and documented what they called the "fierce individualism" of the American people. They concluded that we are a people trained to believe that happiness is what we should seek in life and that happiness is ultimately a matter of individual self-fulfillment. In the words of one of the people they spoke to: "In the end you're really alone, and you really have to answer to yourself." So life is about self-fulfillment, and self-fulfillment happens when you look out for number one above all.

The result of this distorted outlook on life is a very weak commitment to those relationships that ultimately give life meaning. I don't need friends, or if I do, they are dispensable and replaceable, and no one should be kept in my life who does not advance my pursuit of happiness and self-fulfillment.

The same attitude then applies to marriage, to churches, to coworkers and jobs, to local communities. We move through life like isolated atoms, attaching ourselves temporarily and not very deeply to other people and places, replacing these people when they no longer contribute to our happiness or when we can get a better deal somewhere else – or they replace us for the same reasons. And in the end we are horribly alone.

This isolation and individualism are reflected and fostered by other national trends. We are a population in which 17 percent of us move in any given year. That's 42 million people moving every year. The percentages are highest for those under the age of forty, which is most of us in this room. How are we supposed to become close to people when either we or they will likely move within a couple years?

This has been our own pilgrimage as a family. Jeanie and I have lived in five states in thirteen years of marriage. Our oldest daughter was born in New York and has since lived in Raleigh, Philadelphia, Louisville, and now Jackson. Not long ago she rather innocently asked, "When people ask me where I grew up, what should I tell them?" That caught us up short, I can tell you.

Economic insecurity contributes to the need for so many to move, as well as the divorce epidemic, which always results in somebody moving somewhere, at least once.

Thus, many of us find ourselves alone, isolated, perhaps unwilling to easily change our individualism, but with a vague sense that something is not right in our lonely lives.

2. *No one can experience Christian growth in isolation.* Throughout its pages, the Bible assumes that no one can walk with God, can live for God, in isolation.

In the Old Testament, God established a special covenant relationship not with isolated individuals but with the people Israel. It was to the people as a whole that he spoke, to the people that he gave the Law, to the people that he related. "I will be your God, and you shall be my *people*," he said.

When Jesus lived out his earthly ministry, he spoke with individuals, sure. But he invested his primary efforts in that small band of twelve people we know collectively as the disciples. For three years they spent every day with him and with each other. And as he prepared to die for our sins, he told them that they were no longer his servants but his friends, friends he loved to the very end (John 15).

Paul's favorite image for the church is the body of Christ. In 1 Corinthians 12 he offers an extended discussion of the church as the body of Christ, and of each member as a part of that body, analogous to its eyes, ears, hands, ankles, kneecaps, and so on. Notice that a body may have many parts but it is one organism; as Paul said – "If one part suffers, every part suffers with it; if one part is honored, every part rejoices with it" (v. 26).

Many people think that they can do Christianity without church. Bellah and his *Habits of the Heart* team coined the term "Sheilaism" for this view; they named it after a woman they interviewed named Sheila, who said she believed in God but didn't need church and could essentially handle this religion thing on her own. I know many who are this way, many who are among the 90 percent of the American people who say they believe in God but not part of that 40 percent who go to church.

Yet when I talk with such people, I sometimes tell them of my friend Bill's walk away from the Christian faith. Of how he abandoned his ties to his Christian friends and joined himself to another community – a community of books and music and people hostile to Christ. There is no authentic Christianity in isolation.

3. *Therefore, we must choose to invest deeply in meaningful Christian community.* There really is no alternative. If you want to be a Christ follower, you must join yourself with other Christ followers. This investment needs to happen on several levels, which we can picture as concentric circles, one within the other, each taking you deeper into authentic Christian community.

First, every Christian needs to invest deeply in the life of a local body of believers. Keep up the pilgrimage. From occasional visits (Christmas and Easter) to regular attendance; from slipping out the back quickly to talking with people; from visiting around to regularly attending in one place; from regular one-place attending to membership; from membership to joyful fellowship and service. That's the path of progress. Where are you? It doesn't have to be Northbrook; it does have to be somewhere.

Second, every Christian needs to invest deeply in a small group either within that local body of believers or somewhere else within the family of faith. In small groups "everybody knows your name." We lose our anonymity. We experience Christian growth and a context of intimacy and support. Small groups become the context for more extensive Bible study and worship.

Third, every Christian needs to invest deeply in an accountability relationship. This is one-on-one friendship in which you are totally transparent with someone else. It should not be your spouse but instead a same-sex friend who supports, challenges, listens, and holds you accountable. This should be someone either at your same level of maturity or further along. Every Christian needs at least one intimate Christian friend of this type. Do you have one?

Too busy to have relationships of this type? I would argue that you're too busy not to. Such relationships are like the support beams in a house; if they're not there, your house is not well built, and it won't last, no matter how much interesting activity goes on there. Build those support beams into your life. Jesus did.

4. *To invest deeply in Christian community requires us to learn the arts of mutual submission.* What are these arts?

- vulnerability – openness; lowering the walls; allowing yourself to be seen, your weaknesses and sins to be known, your humanity to be obvious. Such self-revelation and self-exposure to others are very frightening, for we fear being exploited, wounded, hurt. Yet the paradox is that there is no intimacy without vulnerability and no community without intimacy. And so we must submit to the dangers of vulnerability to receive the blessings of community. And you know what? There's nobody you can be vulnerable with who is not also human. We all have vulnerabilities and all mess up. It is a great relief to discover this!

- teachability – Matthew 18:15. The New Testament is clear that Christian community requires a willingness to learn from others, even when that learning is through the most painful means of personal rebuke and correction. Here is where our individualism wants to rear its ugly head and roar, "Don't tread on me. Don't tell me what to do." But this is how growth happens, the only way sometimes.

· responsibility – the willingness to meet the needs of others in a compassionate and consistent way by rebuking where that is needed, as in this passage; by standing with the suffering sister or brother; by meeting financial needs in crisis; by praying for one another; by doing whatever love requires in a given situation.

· accountability – Christian community, as the New Testament envisions it, is to consist precisely in this mutual vulnerability, teachability, and responsibility, all exercised in love, trust, and mercy. It leads to a community of strength and resilience, of shared character and shared values, in which everyone agrees that this is what it means to follow Jesus Christ – and everyone is willing to be held accountable for that way of life.

5. *Finally, God uses Christian community in profound ways when we invest deeply in it.*

· for comfort in times of trouble and sorrow.

· for spiritual and moral growth and challenge – as iron sharpens iron, we urge each other on.

· for affirmation of our gifts, calling, and potential roles – people come to know us well enough to see gifts in us we didn't see, to get us involved in roles we never knew we could handle, to open our minds to the calling God may be placing on us.

· for that network of friends that provide the most profound meaning to be found in this life – phone calls and visits, meals together and tears together; hearty belly laughs and heartfelt talks; standing with you in the hospital and you with them at the graveside; those people who with joined hands walk this pilgrim way with us.

· for a context for the advance of God's kingdom. We look up from our own lives and see God's work, God's kingdom purpose in a broken world, and we realize that this bond of Christian community exists not just so my needs get met and your needs get met but primarily so that the needs of God's bruised and broken world get met. The joy of being coworkers for God – this is perhaps the most sublime of all joys.

And so we end where we began: with a call to move from isolation into meaningful Christian community, or to take the next step in your pilgrimage into that community, whatever it might be. Don't do Sheilaism; be a Christian instead. This is my invitation.

Jesus and Santa

Romans 12:1–2

This 1997 sermon attempted to apply distinctively Christian moral thinking to the annual recognition of Christmas and through that to consider our overall relation to culture. Taking off on the categories for the relation between Christ and culture offered by H. Richard Niebuhr some fifty years ago, the sermon works primarily at the principle level. Its immediate context locally included growing controversy among Christians over whether or how to participate in such culturally approved festivals as Halloween. Its strategy involves heavy reference to popular Christmas films and songs in an effort to connect with the unchurched and draw them into the categories of Christian thought. — dpg

Introduction

Forty years ago a theologian named H. Richard Niebuhr wrote a book called *Christ and Culture.* In that book, he laid out five historic Christian patterns for how the church has sought to relate to the world around it. The problem goes something like this: Christians claim to be Christ-followers – to be loyal to Jesus above all else and to be committed to doing what he wants in their lives. And this is what we should be. However, Christians live in cultures like our own that do not universally share that commitment and are sometimes downright hostile to it. So the question is how we navigate between our commitment to

Christ and our unavoidable immersion in the culture in which we live.

This is an issue that comes up all the time as we decide what movies to watch, or whether to watch any movies at all; what products to buy; what clothes to wear; what parts of our bodies to have pierced, if any; what language to use or not use; what values to embrace. Basically, it's a twenty-four-hours-a-day, seven-days-a-week issue for Christians. The issue, as Paul put it, is how to be transformed by the renewing of our minds rather than be conformed to the pattern of this world.

Recently the tensions between Christ and culture have become clearer to American Christians on a wide range of particular issues. One of the most interesting battlegrounds has had to do with how we handle certain holidays. Have you noticed the heightened attention in recent years concerning whether or how Christians should get involved in the observance of Halloween?

Increasingly, thoughtful Christians are asking the same question about Christmas. How shall the Christian relate to the culture at Christmastime? Or, to put it another way, what does Jesus have to do with Santa? I want to adapt Niebuhr's categories to suggest four different ways in which Christians are answering that question right now. I hope that the outcome will not only be some insight concerning how we ought to handle Christmas, but also how we ought to live in our current culture.

Jesus Not Santa

Have you ever seen that sign as you have driven around Jackson? We first noticed it last year. Block lettering, in red, on a rectangular white board: JESUS NOT SANTA.

Jesus not Santa. This category could also be called Jesus against Santa. Someone suggested I call it Jesus Kills Santa, but that is probably a bit harsh. It does, however, communicate the flavor of this position. Some Christians think that the way to relate to the kind of culture in which we live is basically to set ourselves in opposition to it. Culture – at least, late 1990s American culture – is bad, pagan, evil, perverse, and must be rejected. Christ has nothing to do with culture and neither should Christians. As much as possible, we should try to get free of it.

I see two different paths within this option. One is the withdrawal path. Here Christians simply try to build a moat around their Christian castles, pull up the drawbridge, and shut the world out as best they can. Within that castle they seek to remain as pure and undirtied by the influence of culture as they can.

The other path is a more aggressive one. Here Christians declare war on a pagan culture, verbally attack it at every turn, expose its many flaws and sins, and seek to win as many victories against it as possible.

"Jesus Not Santa" would be the Christmastime motto of both of these groups. Some Christians try to withdraw completely from every dimension of the annual Christmas festival that is not explicitly related to the birth of Jesus. In its strongest form, people give no presents, hang no decorations, listen to no secular Christmas music, and have no Santa. The benefit of this approach is its clarity about what Christmas is really about: the birth of the Savior, Jesus Christ. It may be that for some a total withdrawal from the cultural side of Christmas is the best way to make the season be what it ought to be. But this effort to completely close out every dimension of culture, or especially to declare war against it, can lead Christians into a stance toward the world that can only be described as grinch-like. [A clip from the film *The Grinch Who Stole Christmas* was used here.] Sometimes that's how Christians present themselves to society – as grinches.

Jesus Is Santa

I don't think we want to be the grinches of American culture. That's not what God calls his church to be. However, on the opposite end of the spectrum lies the opposite danger. Let's call this the Jesus is Santa position. Niebuhr called it the Christ of culture. Here what happens is that Christians lose any sense that there is or ever could be a conflict between follow-ing Jesus and living in a secular culture. They just go along, do what everybody else is doing, watch what everybody else is watching, think what everybody else is thinking, and mer-rily accommodate themselves to American culture. Sometimes this takes the form of an unhealthy, even unholy, confusion be-tween the things of God and the things of this world. There is enough religiosity left in this culture for people to want to be religious and to use God-talk now and again. But sometimes this cultural religion completely loses its integrity and any contact with the God of the Bible.

Jesus is Santa. A great example of this confusion can be found in one of the verses of the old Christmas favorite "Here Comes Santa Claus." The singer is the old cowboy Gene Autry. Listen closely. [Played the song.] "So let's give thanks to the Lord above, because Santa Claus is coming tonight." Hmmm. Does that strike any other adult in the room as a bit of a problem? So the first problem here is culture religion; Jesus is Santa, Santa is Jesus; he knows if you've been bad or good. Christianity becomes culture.

Perhaps the more common problem today is when the cul-ture completely swallows up what was originally Christian. In the case of Christmas, what emerges is a happy festival that has something to do with giving or "goodwill to men" but nothing to do with Jesus, whose name somehow cannot be said in as-sociation with this festival. Consider the words from one of my favorite Christmas classics, *The Berenstain Bears Meet Santa Bear:* "The most magical thing of all is Santa Bear...because the joy of giving is what Christmas is all about." Oh, really? I thought it had something to do with the birth of the Savior of the world.

Jesus and Santa

Okay. So we're not thrilled about Jesus being at war with Santa. Nor do we want Jesus to become Santa. Are there any other op-tions? I think the third is best labeled "Jesus and Santa." This one may sound promising. But what I mean by Jesus and Santa is this: Some Christians do attend to the Jesus side of Christmas and to the Santa side of Christmas, but the latter appears unaffected by the former. Christ is a part of Christmas, which is a good thing but has not been allowed to have any impact on the cultural side of the Christmas celebration.

Example: Friday, November 28, the day after Thanksgiving. Crowds line up outside Target at 6 A.M. to snatch up the hot Christmas sales. Tempers flare as two lines compete for first crack at the door. The doors open; shoppers rush in to claim their treasures; a woman ends up with a bloody mouth, elbowed by a determined shopper. Is there anything wrong with this picture?

There is a good reason why the cultural celebration of Christmas has been reduced to the message that "the joy of giving is what Christmas is all about." As the old *Saturday Night Live* "Church Lady" would say: "*How convenient* . . . that this message fuels our consumerism; that if the joy of giving is what Christmas is all about, then, by golly, the more giving, the more Christmas; indeed, the more expensive the giving, the more the spirit of the season is honored." It has been rightly said that shopping is in fact the master American passion, the one true national religion. Over $40 billion dollars was made last Christmas in retail sales in this country. An honest appraisal of the culture would tell us that it is the almighty dollar that is the true center of our annual festival.

Here's my claim: It is not enough to throw a little Jesus into Christmas while participating without reflection in the eating, drinking, buying, charging, spending, partying festival that Christmas has become. And the same is true more generally: The Christian faith is not something you lay beside culture and then try to do both. The Christian faith is something that transforms your entire way of life. And this leads us to our last point.

Jesus Transforms Santa

"Do not conform any longer to the pattern of this world, but be transformed by the renewing of your mind. . . . " Jesus transforms Santa, and Christmas, and work, and family life – all of life.

If you hear nothing else this morning, hear that. The first of the Ten Commandments reads: "You shall have no other gods but me." Interesting thing about God: He really does not appreciate having to share worship and devotion with anyone or anything else. We mean the same thing when we say that Jesus is Lord. That means that he is in charge of our lives. We then are obligated – a joyful obligation – to lay every element of our lives at his feet and say, "What do you want me to do with this part of my life?"

And so what would Christmas look like if we did that? If we said, "Jesus, the one whose birth we celebrate this month, what do you want me – or our family – to do with Christmas this year? Because you are the Lord and Leader of my life, just tell me, and I'll do it." Thoughtful Christians, having asked just such a question, are coming up with some very interesting ideas. Just about everyone recognizes that consumerism is the chief idol that threatens the lordship of Christ at Christmas. So some are giving all gift money to missions instead; others are setting strict dollar limits on giving and giving the rest to God's work in the world. One writer last year proposed that families establish a maximum of $100 in total Christmas spending no matter how much they could spend.

Along with this approach, some Christians are looking for ways to show Christ's love at Christmas. What better way to honor his birth is there than this? These Christians are serving food at soup kitchens, visiting shut-ins and those in nursing homes, and putting together food baskets and gifts for needy families.

Another approach is to try to make space for the celebration of family love. Some are turning off the TV, saying no to many Christmas party invitations, and instead devoting the season to spending more time with one another, recording family trees, and generally investing in family life.

Most important, Jesus transforms Santa when space is made for quiet reflection on Jesus himself and on our relationship with him. Our family has adopted the tradition of the Advent candles and the reading of Scriptures related to the birth of Christ.

Being a Christ follower doesn't necessarily mean embracing any particular one of these ideas. It does mean that in this season of the year, as in every season, Jesus is Lord and Leader, and we are his followers, seeking to be transformed in our minds and in our lives and to do his good, pleasing, and perfect will.

New Passages:
Life in the Spirit
Ephesians 2:1–10

Our year-long 1996 theme at Walnut Street was "Turn Your Eyes upon Jesus." The year was broken into various segments allowing the theme to develop along different paths. In April the theme development centered on the work of the Holy Spirit. This message examined the difference between being Spirit-empowered and merely human-powered in the Christian life. This was an effort to get at the spiritual resources that undergird the entire Christian moral life. The sermon also includes an effort to explore the character trait of humility. — rhl

They were known as V-2 rockets. The Germans developed them during the latter days of the Second World War. Though exotic weapons, they never proved to be of much value to Germany's war effort. Combined with German experimentation with heavy water (the first stage of nuclear weapons development), the V-2 rockets took enormous amounts of German resources at the expense of other weapons systems more valuable to the war effort. Today many historians believe Hitler's fixation on exotic weapons caused him to give up the greatest single tactical advantage he would ever have. You see, the Germans had already developed jet propulsion – but because Hitler spent all of his resources on the development of rocketry and of the heavy water experiments that would lead to atomic weapons, he had no resources left to develop jet engines and put them on his military planes – until the very end of the war when it was too late. Why? Most likely because he did not know the power of the engine he had at his disposal.

You and I have a similar problem as Christians. Every day we have the opportunity to live our lives propelled by the Spirit of God. Yet too often Christians give up this single greatest advantage to instead live life pushed along by the same old engine. Now if you are lost, if you do not know Christ as your Savior, you don't have any choice. You only have one engine. But if you are a Christian, it is a shame that you would give up the empowerment of the Spirit to instead putt-putt along with what you can do as a human being.

I have often wondered why it is that we would give up such a marvel in order to accept what is clearly second-rate. Part of it is because we never truly understand what it means to be humble. Now listen carefully. The world says, "Ah, humility, that's a wonderful attitude." The world says that humility is an attitude of submissive deference to others. It sees humility as when we put others' needs or cares or concerns above our own. To the world, humility means you are meek and mild; in other words, very easy to get along with. The world thinks that being humble means there's not much maintenance to you.

The world doesn't really understand what it means to be humble. Because before anyone can have an attitude that reflects humility, one must first of all understand the relationship that creates humility. Hear me clearly. What the world tries to pawn off as humility is an absolutely artificial waste of time. You can't be the world's kind of humble unless you just happen to be somebody that lets other folks walk all over you. You are not by nature necessarily humble. And if you can conjure up the attitude, it's artificial at best.

Humility from the biblical standpoint has to do with understanding my relationship to the world. I understand that God is the creator and I am the creation. I understand that the world doesn't revolve around me. I understand that I am a part of what God has made. Even the English word *humility* comes from a background that says that we are of the earth. I cannot adopt an attitude of humility until I first understand the relationship that creates it. The reason why many Christians never allow the Spirit of God to empower their lives is because they have never understood nor come to rest in that relationship. Do you remember the words of the classic hymn, "All creatures of our God and King, lift up our voice and let us sing"? When I understand my relationship as creature to God as creator and rest in that relationship, I become a humble individual. Is there an advantage in that? You had better believe it. Can you and I have that advantage in our lives? I am convinced that we can.

I want us to look at the two engines that are available to us. The first engine is that one with which we came into the world. By it, we are driven by human forces. We are very good at covering up and masking its hollowness. We are very skilled at making it look very clear and very beautiful and very, very desirable. So first of all, when you look at this engine, you have to strip away the mask. When you do, you will be surprised to discover that once you strip away all pretense, you are dead and dominated.

Listen once again to the words the apostle Paul used: "You were dead in your transgressions and sins, in which you used to live" (Ephesians 2:1-2). Why and how? "When you followed the ways of this world and of the ruler of the kingdom of the air." Not only were we dead but we were dominated. Everyone you know – no matter how good he or she is, no matter how outstanding he or she might be as a personality – everyone you know who is outside of God's grace has a life that is putting along by this kind of engine. Such people are dead and dominated. You were that way the Scripture says. Why in the world would we want to go back and live that way again? It is beyond me. I suppose we have masked all of the death in that old engine.

The poet Oscar Wilde wrote a line that may very well be his spiritual epitaph. He said, "I ceased to be lord over myself. I was no longer the captain of my soul. I allowed desire to dominate me. I ended in horrible disgrace." Friends, that person you think is just a fine, fine example of humanity except for being outside of Christ – Wilde's description is of him. That's her. That's the description of how they will end their lives. Horrible. What a waste!

Whenever you buy a car, you want to know how much power it has, so you ask a lot of questions. I have come to a

point in my life where I no longer desire to push the acceler-
ator all the way to the floor and hold it there. I did do that at
one time, but I finally developed some brains along the way.
But even now when I go to look at a car I ask what kind of
horsepower it has. (Like I'm going to find out and use it all.) I
want to know how many miles it will go on a tank of gas. (Like
I'm going to try and find out if it will go exactly that number of
miles.) We always want to know what the capacity is.

Let's look at the capacity of the engine that drives most
of the lives you know. Verse 1 says that being dead in transgressions and sins is a defeated lifestyle. It is mind-numbing,
life-sapping defeat. Not only that, it is a life that is absolutely
given over to desires that ultimately end in destroying us. In
verse 3 we find how all of us also lived at one time, gratifying
the cravings of our sinful nature. That is the capacity of the
best people we know, outside of Christ. Sadly, many Christians
are living with that kind of an engine propelling their lives.
Is it any wonder why folks barely look at our witness in their
presence?

I also want to know when I look at an engine what its final
results are going to be. When I choose as a Christian to live my
life propelled by this kind of an engine, I find myself estranged
from the very one who gives me life. I am left with a strained
relationship to God. All because I wanted to see if I could run
things on my own. Folks, there is a better way. The Bible tells
us that there is a better engine by which to propel our lives,
and it is available to those who have been born again.

It is a life empowered by God's Spirit. Those of you who
have been born again, this is the way you ought to live your
life. This is the way you *can* live your life. Before we live life
that way, we're going to have to understand that true humility
isn't some kind of meek and mild attitude; it is a reflection of
our relationship with God. I know who God is, and I know how
I relate to him. The attitude becomes a part of the relationship.
When that happens, we begin to get into a position where the
Spirit of God empowers us so that our lives are different. But
before you are going to trust God that way, you are going to
have to understand something of his motives.

Listen to the fourth verse. "Because of his great love for us,

God, ... is rich in mercy." Isn't that amazing? That is the kind of God we serve. You want to know about God's motives where you are concerned? You need to remember only two words – love and mercy. These are the motives that propel God whenever he thinks about you – and not just you, but everyone you know.

Not only do we need to know something about God's motive but we need to discover something of God's plan. Verses 8-10 tell us that it is by grace that we have been saved through faith; this is not of ourselves, not something we do. Paul goes on to say that we are God's handiwork, the work of his hands. You and me. That's God's plan – to save us and make us the craftsmanship of his creative energies. You are not saved and shelved. You have been saved; you have been brought into God's kingdom to be elevated to a beautiful place. You are God's handiwork created for a purpose. And that purpose is that you would come alive and reign with Christ in heavenly places.

That is the kind of engine that can drive your life. And, my friends, when that kind of engine does drive your life, people take notice. Some of you today need to be saying, "I am sick and tired of putting along with an engine that doesn't get me anywhere. I'm sick and tired of my life not being a reflection of my relationship to God." Today, my friends, you may need to make some changes. Make this the day you make a fresh start and begin to live in the power of God's Spirit.

Race Relations:
A Biblical Perspective
Ephesians 2:14–19

*This 1994 sermon was preached to a Louisville congre-
gation of which I was a lay member. The generic title
reflects the fact that this sermon was offered on "Race
Relations Sunday," one of the several moral emphasis
Sundays in Southern Baptist life. These days provide the
only structured annual opportunity available in our denomination to address the kinds of moral issues that
are the focus of this volume. Despite progress in recent years, race continues to be a besetting problem in
our churches and in our nation. The sermon primarily focuses on the theological framework level, this time
using the doctrinal rather than narrative style. The application section works on the principle level while also
offering concrete "rule-like" exhortations. It is clearly targeted to Christians and seeks to make application on
individual, congregational, and societal levels. — dpg*

Introduction

I'd like to begin by telling you a story that a student told me
last semester. I had been lecturing in my Christian ethics intro
class on racism. Afterward one of my students, a distinguished-
looking African man in his late thirties, came up to me. His
eyes were glistening. As I remember it, this is what he said:

Three years ago I came to this country to pursue my education. I was all alone and living in one of the major cities of the South. It was wintertime and very, very cold. On my first Sunday in town I wanted to go to church, because I have been a Christian for many years. I didn't have a car, so I buttoned up my rather thin coat and started walking. I planned to attend the nearest church.

After a three-mile walk, I finally found a church. It happened to be a Baptist church, which pleased me, because I am a Baptist. Relieved to be getting out of the cold at last, I stepped inside the church building and started looking for the sanctuary.

I found it and was about to find a seat for the service. However, some men at that church saw me and began walking toward me. One of them gestured that I should follow him out of the sanctuary and back into the hall. I did. When we got back out there, he told me that I had to leave. I was stunned. I asked him, "Why?" He said that black people were not allowed to attend services at that church.

I was completely surprised. I had never experienced anything like this in my life. No one had warned me that this could happen. I turned around and walked out of the church. I was devastated. I buttoned up my coat and began the three-mile walk back to my apartment.

The Biblical Case Against Racism

I hope you are as grieved by this story as I was when I heard it. And there's good reason to be grieved – because what the men of that church did to this African student that day was fundamentally contrary to the teachings of the Bible.

The biblical case against racism is based on three pillars: creation, the cross, and the church. Let's take each of them in turn.

1. Creation

First, creation. We read in Genesis 1:27:

> *So God created man in his own image,*
> *in the image of God he created him;*
> *male and female he created them.*

Once Paul was preaching to a skeptical bunch of listeners in the ancient Greek capital city of Athens. He spoke to them of the one God "who made the world and everything in it" (Acts 17:24). Paul went on to say that it was this same God who from one ancestor (Adam) made all nations to inhabit the whole earth (v. 26). All of us are, in Paul's words, "God's offspring" (v. 28).

Adolf Hitler, leader of the German Nazi party, was one who didn't believe this. Hitler believed that there are Aryans and there are Jews, and they come from different gods – the Jews' god being inferior, of course.

But what the Bible teaches is that there is only one God, and this God is the Father of us all. And if we are all God's children, then our children are right when they sing to us, "Red and yellow, black and white, all are precious in his sight." Every person and group of people is of immense worth to God. There can be no biblical justification for believing that some groups of people are more valuable in God's sight than others. And if all groups are equal in God's sight, they must be in ours as well.

2. Cross

The second pillar of the biblical case against racism is found in the cross of Jesus Christ. We see Paul make this argument in our text this evening. His subject is the uneasy relationship between Jews and Gentiles. For centuries in the ancient world, Jews and non-Jews (called Gentiles) had treated each other coldly if not contemptuously. Jews wouldn't associate with Gentiles, and Gentiles returned the favor. Jews thought Gentiles were pagans, and Gentiles thought the Jews' religion was strange. Jews didn't like Gentile culture, and Gentiles didn't like Jewish culture. And on it went. We see the Jew-Gentile tension throughout much of the New Testament.

Paul is remarking on this tension in our passage. He talks about the ancient "dividing wall of hostility between us" – that is, between Jews and Gentiles. But Paul makes a remarkable series of claims: "Christ is our peace." "He has broken down the dividing wall of hostility." Christ's purpose is to create in himself one new humanity where once there were two. As he hung on the cross, he was putting to death this ancient hostility. So the cross is not only about reconciling sinners with God; it is, in Paul's view, about reconciling sinful groups with each other.

Think about the cross for a minute. There is an old saying you may have heard: "Everyone stands equal at the foot of the cross." Why? Because it is the sin of every human being, bar none, and every human group, bar none, that nailed Jesus to the cross. And it is on behalf of every human being and every human group that he died. Jesus is "Savior of the world."

What all of this means is that Jesus Christ and the cross belong to everyone. Christ is not the Savior of white people only, as the KKK seems to think; he is the Savior of everyone who believes. Praise God, no one is left out.

3. Church

This brings us to the third pillar of the case against racism: the nature and purpose of the church. After talking about the reconciling work of Christ on the cross, Paul, in verse 19, moves on to talk about what this means for the church. He says, "You [Gentiles] are no longer strangers and aliens, but you are citizens with the saints . . . and members of the household of God." The old Jewish-Gentile dividing wall has been overcome; in the church all are members of the household of God.

So this is the nature of the church: a new humanity in which worldly barriers drop away, and we see that in Christ there is neither Jew nor Greek, slave nor free, male nor female – we are simply one in Christ Jesus, as Paul wrote (Galatians 3:28).

And this is the purpose of the church: to "make disciples of all nations," the Great Commission. In Revelation 14 the apostle John talked about an angel who flew about with an "eternal gospel to proclaim to those who live on the earth – to every nation, tribe, language and people" (v. 6).

The church is to be a community that is not only willing but eager to welcome all kinds of people into its midst. For us, worldly differences are to fade completely out of the picture. When people join us on Sunday morning, they are either fellow Christians who are to be welcomed gladly as brothers and sisters in Christ; or they are people in need of Christ to whom we are commanded to bear witness in the name of Christ. Either way, whoever walks in our door must be welcomed without reservation.

What Is Racism?

So what happened that day? Why did the Christians of that Southern Baptist church treat my student friend as they did? They did so because they were in bondage to racism. That bondage overrode their loyalty to Christ. Racism does that to people. Basically, racism is a horribly distorted way of responding to something we notice very early in life: People are different from one another. To make it personal – other people are different from *me*. They have different color skin. Their eyes, hair, and faces look different. They speak different languages. They are from different nations or ethnic groups. They prefer different kinds of food, music, and art.

Racism develops when these differences are seen as a *problem*. It happens when we look around us and conclude that "your kind is different from my kind, and my kind is better." We don't have to respond to difference in this way. We could notice that humanity does consist of a number of different kinds of people and conclude that this is a wonderful sign of God's creativity, even of his love – that we should be blessed with so many different kinds of people to get to know. But racism doesn't see it this way. It tends to organize the world into my (superior) kind of people and your (inferior) kind of people. This in itself is wrong in God's eyes. But the situation worsens when people, as individuals or groups, act on these beliefs. They treat members of other groups as inferior. They won't associate with them – in school, work, church, or community. They humiliate and mistreat them in a million petty ways. This is what happened that cold winter day to my African friend.

And this is small potatoes in comparison with the large-scale, violent, and systematic expression of racism that so often occurs. Friday we learned of the mass murder of Muslim Arabs in Hebron as they knelt in prayer in a mosque. The man who did it, Baruch Goldstein, was a Jewish racist. A "Jewish racist" – the term itself is a tragedy, because it has been the Jewish people through the centuries who have faced some of the worst racism the world has seen, including its ultimate expression, the Holocaust.

We see the effects of racism in Bosnia and in many other places around the world, as well as in our own nation. As the pastor wrote in his column this week, quoting Billy Graham: "Racial and ethnic hostility is the foremost social problem facing our world today."

Conclusion: What Must We Do?

If we believe, as we must, that racism is contrary to the Word of God, what must we do? We need to work against it. *In our own hearts*, we need to ask God to rid us of racism. We may have been raised that way or picked it up along the way, but in any case, we need to ask God to free us from it. We need to renounce racist actions while God works to free our hearts of racist attitudes. Racism hurts the racist as well as the victim of racism. It is a bondage that keeps us from serving our Lord Jesus.

In our church, we need to be completely clear that we will not do what that church did that day. We simply won't disobey Christ in that way. We will be color-blind in reaching out to our community and warm in welcoming all who come our way. We will not make racial distinctions at any level of our church's life. Our commission is to "make disciples of *all nations*." That's what we will do.

We can consider further steps. We could try a pulpit exchange with a minister from a black church. Or we could invite a choir from a downtown church here and send our choir there. We could undertake a joint service project with a minority congregation. If walls are truly to be broken down, they won't come down by themselves.

In society, we can resist any politician who tries to win votes by inflaming racial divisions. We can support enforcement of fair housing laws. We can work for equal educational opportunities for all of God's children. We can oppose any form of illegal but still common discrimination against minorities in hotels, restaurants, and the like. There is much to be done. We just have to decide if we're in the game, and if so, which team we're on.

Paul wrote: "[Christ] is our peace, who has made the two one and has destroyed the barrier, the dividing wall of hostility." Let's be a part of Christ's work – the tearing down, rather than the building up, of the walls that divide us from one another.

Why Can't I Have It All?

1 Thessalonians 4:3–7; 2 Timothy 4:9–13

This 1997 sermon examines the character issue of whether God wants Christian people to be happy or holy. It accomplishes its goal through a character study of the obscure New Testament figure named Demas. The sermon focuses relentlessly on the single question under consideration and does so through the unique means of a negatively oriented character study. — rhl

On June 4, 1942, the balance of power in the entire world was changed in five minutes. I find that an incredible fact. The United States navy, crippled by a surprise attack only months before, had managed to break their enemies' military code. As a result, it was now lying in wait to take on the Japanese navy, one of the most powerful military forces in the world. The American strategic planners had decided to gamble and try to somehow even the odds and begin to throttle that great power, Japan. They decided on a coordinated attack, but before all of the planes had been launched that morning, the attack had already disintegrated through a combination of mechanical failures and incomplete and, in some cases, inaccurate information about the enemies' whereabouts and strength. Even some bad staff decisions in planning reduced the attack to an uncoordinated collection of coincidences. As a result, forty-one of the slowest and most vulnerable planes in the American fleet were forced to take on the Japanese navy singlehandedly. They were called torpedo bombers, and that simply meant that they flew very close to the surface of the water. They had to go straight in toward the target, and in order to be able to accomplish this

191

with any chance of surviving, they had to depend on American fighter planes to help them and American dive bombers to coordinate their attack and at least draw some of the enemies' attention off them. But on this morning, because of the series of blunders, they were on their own – forty-one virtually defenseless planes. Thirty-five of them would end up in the water and with the planes nearly seventy young men would perish.

If you study this battle – it is called the Battle of Midway – you will discover something quite interesting about the planes and their men. All of those planes were destroyed, and all of those men were lost, and not one of their weapons found its way to its target. But because they were willing to give themselves up for something they believed more significant than life itself, they drew all the enemies' attention to themselves on the surface of the ocean, and by what military historians call sheer coincidence, the American dive bombers fell from the sky and destroyed four of Japan's aircraft carriers in five minutes' time. History now says that the balance of power in the world shifted in that five-minute span, and it did so because of some incredible young men.

History has recorded their names. We know who they are. And I suspect that now, even fifty-some years after the fact, you could go and find some family members who knew and remember those young men. They were men filled with hopes and dreams, just like you. They were men who believed and hoped and most likely prayed that they would survive not only that day and that battle but the war also, and go home to live out those hopes and dreams. They didn't. They were young men who wanted something out of life just like you want things out of life. What is incredible about their story is that they were willing to give themselves for something more significant than themselves. You can go and do all kinds of research on them, but you don't really have to.

Instead, I can tell you one thing about them that is probably the most pertinent fact of all. There wasn't a Demas in the bunch. I'm not talking about the name. I'm talking about the character. Three times the New Testament records for us the activities of a man named Demas. New Testament scholars believe each reference to be to the same man.

The first two times you encounter Demas, he is a part of Paul's entourage and a follower of Christ. He is a coworker with Paul, helping to build the missionary enterprise. In these first two instances, he is named with others in Paul's company. Only one sentence is given to his story in each of these passages. But now we come to the third time he is mentioned in the New Testament. Paul is now an old man. In the verses I read to you out of 2 Timothy he says, and I paraphrase, "I fought a good fight, I have finished my course, I have kept the faith, and I am now about ready to be given up." And then he says, in some of the most touching of all words in the New Testament, "Do what you can, Timothy, to come to me. Demas has deserted me." Demas is mentioned in the most unflattering of lights. "Demas has deserted me." Many times in the New Testament we are left to conjecture as to what has happened. We are left to try to decide, if we can, what is going on in the passage.

But in this particular instance that is not the case. We are told explicitly why Demas deserted the apostle: He loved the things of this world. Do you not realize that we are a society that glorifies the attitude of Demas? From the moment of your birth until the time of your death, you are bombarded with subtle and not-so-subtle messages that say to you, "You can have it all. You deserve it all. You ought to have what you want." Why can't I have it all? It is a question we ask so often, because even inside houses of worship today, there are folks standing in pulpits saying that God wants you to have it all. Well, at the risk of offending you, let me set the record straight. No, he doesn't. You can turn through the pages of the New Testament many times and you will not find that message. It is not there.

The question of the hour is a simple one. Does God want you to be happy, or does God want you to be holy? I am speaking specifically to Christians, because it is an important issue for you and for me. Many times we look at the Bible and we develop from its pages models for us to measure our lives by. Most of those times the models are very healthy and inspiring ones. But I have discovered there is a great value in sometimes taking an unhealthy model, an unworthy model, and measuring myself by it. When you do, you are going to discover that in Demas you have a most unworthy model. I don't really believe that

Demas deserted Paul on a whim. I don't believe that he woke up one day and suddenly decided that he no longer wanted to serve Christ. I don't believe that is how Demas approached things. I believe that subtly, over time, Demas had been measuring what he wanted out of life and what he suspected God wanted with his life, and he began to discover, as we are taught in our culture time and time again, that he wanted to opt out of doing that which God wanted in favor of doing that which he wanted to do.

We have most of our teenagers sitting in the center section of the balcony. They are beginning to discover, or over the last few years have discovered, their sexuality. They hear every day in the songs we listen to on the radio, in the television shows we watch, in the movies we go to, that our sexuality is our own, that we ought to use it to enhance and enjoy our life. We ought to use it as we use every other part of our life in order to somehow make ourselves happy. Is it any wonder then that our teenagers who happen to be Christians so often wonder what it is that God would really want them to know and do? They hear those messages day after day: "Be happy. Enjoy your life. Express yourself. It's your life." But that is the most unworthy model you can have. Too often those same teenagers look at us. They see us investing all our lives, all our time, all our energy, every ounce of our resources in the same quest, not somehow to find a way to be holy, but rather to be happy. And we think somehow that is our right. Just be happy. There are even preachers who say, "Why, don't you know that God wants you to be happy?" Remember the model of Demas. God doesn't want you to be happy. God wants you to be holy.

Holy is an interesting word. In the Old Testament, where we are originally introduced to the word *holy*, it is reserved for God alone. In the Hebrew, the word means "separate, other than, apart from." Do you know that in the Old Testament the dominant characteristic of God is not love but holiness? When the Israelites began to worship God, they recognized that God was different from anything else they had encountered or understood. They recognized that God was set apart from, other than. All the rules they could use in every other aspect of life simply did not apply where God was concerned.

But over the passage of time, *holiness* began to take on a different definition. By the New Testament era, it still meant separate or set apart, but it also came to apply to how we live. In other words, it developed a moral connotation. Now, all of a sudden, God is not the only one called holy. You as a child of God are also instructed to be holy. In one of Paul's earliest works, his first letter to the church at Thessalonica, he says that God has called us to be holy (4:7). He says that within the context of how we choose to live our lives. In other words, you are set apart and must demonstrate your holiness. You demonstrate that you are different than the rest of the world by the choices that you make. God says you are to be holy as God is holy.

Setting happiness as a goal is unhealthy. That is really what the world has done. It has told us that happiness ought to be the focus of our life. Yet this leads us inevitably to selfishness. Think about it for a moment. When all we concern ourselves with is our own personal happiness, everyone around us is at best either something that we use to get what we want or someone in our way keeping us from what we want. The Bible never says that happiness is a goal worthy of giving our life to. It never once suggests that what you and I should do is to try to figure out some entertaining, engaging, enterprising way to be happy. This is an unworthy and unrealistic goal not worth our time and effort. I don't know how many of us could look around and see people who have given up the best they had, who have given up the choicest gifts of life, who have squandered and wasted so much of what they could have been because they gave themselves over to a headlong pursuit of happiness.

The irony is that when I am so selfish and consumed with what I want, I squeeze life and its good things so hard that when I look at them again, they have either evaporated or become worthless. If we were to take an inventory of this room right now, we could go around and see how many of us would be able to stand up and say, "I thought happiness was the number-one goal in life. I thought that was what I should give myself to, how I should live my life. And I pursued it. I spent my time, energy, and youth on it. I gave it my love and attention. Then when I got what I thought I wanted, I found out how worthless it was." I can't help but wonder how many Demases would have turned their planes around in 1942 and gone back because of the cost they were unwilling to pay. I can't help but wonder how many times children of God have been like Demas, walking with the Lord to a point, but over time allowing the desire for the things of this world to strip them of a living and vital relationship with the Lord Jesus. There is nothing more pitiful in the world than to sit and look at someone who should have walked with the Lord but instead gave himself or herself to the quest for what this world has to offer.

Here's the secret. Happiness isn't obtained when we seek it as a goal. Happiness comes as a by-product of something else. God's plan is that you discover your happiness *through* holiness. No, it is not that God wants you to be an old prude who disapproves of everything good and fun in life. That is not God. God wants you to search and fill that unfilled need that is in you – that need to be holy. God doesn't want you to be miserable; he wants you to discover happiness through holiness. And God always puts holiness in a moral context when he calls us to it.

I want us to do an inventory of our lives this morning. Let us determine in three areas of our lives whether we are moving toward holiness or whether we are trying to pursue happiness.

1. How do you use your time? I have discovered that where I give my time, where I place my energies, where I choose to invest myself, is highly significant. It demonstrates what is a priority to me and what is not.

2. Where do you put your money? We use money as a tool to achieve the things we think are important. When happiness is important to you, you spend your money like you spend your time – trying to get the things you want.

3. How do you express yourself sexually? Whether you are young or old or in between, it makes no difference until the day you die, both physically and psychologically you are still a sexual being. How do you use your sexuality? It says a lot about whether or not you are trying to pursue holiness or happiness.

Does God want you to be happy? Well, as a matter of fact, he does. God figured out a long time ago that you won't be happy when happiness is your sole goal in life. God wants you to be happy as you live a holy life. I'm not playing with words here. Some of you are sitting there saying that you have never been happy or holy. I know. You haven't been happy because that was what you sought. You looked for it in the worst places imaginable. You haven't been holy because you loved the things of this world more than the things of God. Ironically, happiness is best discovered through holiness. And for some of you today it is time to say, "I need a change." You can find true happiness through a holy life devoted to Jesus Christ, the holy one.

Why Be Good?

1 John 4:16–19

This 1997 sermon was first preached in one of the numerous county-seat towns that dot the landscape of west Tennessee. It is purposely simpler in its structure and language than many of my sermons, yet it deals with a very important foundational question in Christian ethics: Why be good? It seemed particularly appropriate to address this theological/moral question in the context of a region in which the moral expectations of Christianity are widely understood yet the reason for those expectations may not be. The intended audience is definitely Christian, and the sermon seeks to speak primarily to individuals. — dpg

Introduction

Last year a student in one of my ethics classes walked into my office, sat down, and asked me point blank, "Why be good?" He went on to say: "I know you teach us all about what Christians are supposed to do and not do. But you haven't really told us why."

He's not the only one who has asked that question. Perhaps you have as well. When temptations of all kinds assail us, when our own weaknesses beset us from within, when the heavens seem silent and it is hard to imagine that anyone is watching us as we go about our lives, . . . *why be good?*

Today I want to propose an answer to that question in two

forms: First I'll offer three false answers, three misplaced reasons you or I may sometimes offer to the "Why be good?" question. Then I'll offer three true answers: one from Jesus in Matthew, one from Paul, and one from John. All complement one another.

Three False Answers

1. We hope to look good before others.

Many times Christians and others act as we do because of what our parents taught us. We are good because they told us to be good. We are good because we must never embarrass the family under any circumstances. Many of us can attest to the power of these expectations.

Sometimes it's not so much parents as it is a broader cultural morality. Of course, this is truer of those in my parents' 1930s generation than in my own 1960s era. But for many people, conventional morality passed on to us by our culture remains a powerful influence. We are good because it is what those around us expect of us.

This remains an especially powerful force in the church setting, the setting we find ourselves in this morning. Church is where the expectations are highest and the sanctions for violating those expectations are most severe. So in church, of all places, we must at least give the appearance of morality and uprightness.

You and I both know the emptiness of all this. If we are good to please our parents or to avoid the wrath of culture or church, or just to seem respectable, our goodness is not real. It may be powerful and may keep us out of trouble sometimes, but it doesn't go to the heart of why we should live moral lives.

Jesus addressed this very question in the Sermon on the Mount. If you look at Matthew 6, you see that he had harsh words for those who sought to give the appearance of piety in order to look good before people. He knew that then, like now, people were tempted to do just that.

Folks, let me tell you, the facade of goodness cannot be kept up indefinitely. We may be able to fool some of the people some of the time, but it can't last. And I can tell you from my ministry with college students that there is one group we're definitely not fooling: our kids. Just the other day one of my students was telling me of the abuse, misery, and finally collapse of her chairman-of-the-deacons kind of family. I was moved as she said, "We looked good on Sunday morning, but we were dying inside." Is this you? Is this your story?

2. We fear hell.

Some of us are "good," more or less anyway, because we continue to carry with us the image of God as the fearsome divine Judge — the "sinners in the hands of an angry God" picture. We are desperately afraid that God might reject us eternally, even consign us to a terrible eternal punishment, and so we toe the line. God is the one we fear.

There is no denying the scriptural teaching that we are indeed sinners, that God does get angry at our sin, and that there is an eternal destiny apart from God. But the New Testament does not teach that we can avoid that eternal destiny by a good life. Instead, as we read in Romans 10:9–13 and elsewhere, eternal salvation is grounded in God's decision to save sinners through the death of Jesus on the cross. Trust in God and belief in Jesus is the foundation of salvation, which then works itself out in a lifetime of discipleship and obedience.

Do you walk in daily fear of hell if you get out of line? Is that why you live the way you do?

3. We want to earn God's acceptance.

The flip side of the fear of hell is the hope of earning God's acceptance. Here the notion is that if I can just live a good enough life, God will love and accept me both here and hereafter. So I'll just try a little bit harder, and maybe if I try hard enough, I'll be good enough.

Not long ago I counseled with a student who had this understanding of God. Susie was a Christian, she said, but no one had ever told her that the Christian life was anything other than the lifelong quest to earn God's acceptance. What made it harder for Susie was that she had never received the acceptance of her own earthly father, and so it was hard for her to even understand the acceptance available to her from God the heavenly Father.

The truth of the matter is found in the New Testament. In Romans 3:10–12 we read that not one of us is righteous. No one. All of us have to rely on God's grace and love; we can't earn acceptance or salvation. We have to let that striving go and simply trust God. This is something we can understand if we are at all self-aware. When we examine ourselves, we can't help but notice that our sinfulness is ineradicable. It is ever before us. The great mystics and saints of the church have always been the ones most aware of the depths of their sin. Yet they have also learned to let go of their striving and to trust in God's forgiveness. And so let it go.

Three True Answers

1. Jesus in the Gospels: Be good to advance God's kingdom.

Jesus said to all who would follow him: "Seek first his kingdom and his righteousness, and all these things will be given to you as well" (Matthew 6:33).

The kingdom of God is the total reign of God; the doing of God's will in your heart and motives, in your family, in your work, in Union City, in America, in the world. It has to do with winning people to Christ, defeating evil, feeding the hungry, slowing the divorce epidemic, routing everything contrary to God's will, and doing God's will.

One reason to be good, then, is so that you might be a usable part of Christ's kingdom-advancing efforts. That God might use you to win people to Christ, to change society, to do his will in the most difficult circumstances. To take back some of the territory that has been lost to sin. Once you have caught a vision of the kingdom, you will want to do nothing to stand in the way of that kingdom. You become a kingdom person. That's a real good reason to be good.

2. Paul: *Be good because you are baptized Christians.*

As Paul says in Romans 6:1–4, to be baptized is to be buried with Christ in his death – to become dead to self and sin. And it is to be raised to spiritual life, not just in heaven but right now. Baptism signals the flowing of resurrection power through your very self.

A baptized Christian is a transformed person. Newness of life is in every dimension. This is what it means to be a baptized Christian. You – I – have died. Christ now lives in and through us. And we are thus, paradoxically, more alive than we ever have been.

Moral transformation is part of this – a key part. Nowhere in the New Testament is it even conceivable that a Christian convert will be anything other than a morally transformed person. Conversion, signaled in baptism, means a new way of life. So why be good? Because it reflects nothing less than the meaning of your baptism.

3. John: *Be good because you love God.*

As we see throughout 1 John, God is love in his very nature. Believers are people who have realized just how profoundly true this is and have begun to experience that love. Believers are astonished that God loves us. This is the foundation for everything else.

Being loved so profoundly, we are moved to love in response. We love because he first loved us. We love God; we love our church family; we love our biological family; indeed, we seek to act in love to all people, all because God first loved us. Our heart is moved; we want to respond to such incredible divine love by imitation. Thus, we seek to live in a way that will be pleasing to him. Why be good? Because God loves us and we love God.

Conclusion

I am struck by a profound parallel between our subject and romantic love. Bear with me as I conclude with that parallel.

I don't act rightly in relation to my wife in order to look good before the neighbors or even before her. I don't act rightly toward my wife because I fear the hellish consequences if I fail to do so. Perfect love casts out fear. Fear is not what motivates me. I don't act rightly toward my wife because I want to earn her acceptance. She has already accepted me. That is the foundation of our relationship, not the outcome.

Instead, I act the way I do toward my wife because I love her and because she loves me. I want to please her for this reason. It is also true that I act charitably and lovingly toward her because doing so advances the purposes for which our marriage relationship was established. And it is inconceivable for me to act in any other way simply because I find this way of living to be built into the meaning of the marriage relationship into which I have been, one might say, baptized.

All of this reflects the message of the New Testament concerning our relationship with God. It really is good news. God loves you, and he demonstrated that love on the cross. He wants you to come to him and love him in response – not to live a superficially good life so you don't embarrass yourself, not to relate to him in anxious fear of hell or in an endless search for his acceptance.

No. Love him. Live in resurrection power. And join him in his divine project on this earth – the advance of his kingdom. It's a glorious way to live, and it is preparation for an even more glorious eternity spent loving the God who first loved us.